Critical Pedagogical Narratives of Long-Term Incarcerated Juveniles

Critical Pedagogical Narratives of Long-Term Incarcerated Juveniles

Humanizing the Dehumanized

Gregory Barraza

LEXINGTON BOOKS
Lanham • Boulder • New York • London

Published by Lexington Books
An imprint of The Rowman & Littlefield Publishing Group, Inc.
4501 Forbes Boulevard, Suite 200, Lanham, Maryland 20706
www.rowman.com

86-90 Paul Street, London EC2A 4NE

British Library Cataloguing in Publication Information Available

Library of Congress Cataloging-in-Publication Data

Names: Barraza, Gregory, 1971- author.
   Title: Critical pedagogical narratives of long-term incarcerated juveniles
      : humanizing the dehumanized / Gregory Barraza.
   Description: Lanham : Lexington Books, [2023] | Includes bibliographical
      references and index. | Summary: "Critical Pedagogical Narratives of
      Long-Term Incarcerated Juveniles: Humanizing the Dehumanized uses short
      fictive narratives and poetry of currently and formerly incarcerated
      juveniles. It gives an in-depth look at influences that affect their
      trajectory on the School to Prison Pipeline, and how their experiences
      interrelate with their educational experience"-- Provided by publisher.
   Identifiers: LCCN 2022036911 (print) | LCCN 2022036912 (ebook) | ISBN
      9781666912944 (cloth) | ISBN 9781666912968 (paper) | ISBN
9781666912951 (epub)
   Subjects: LCSH: Juvenile delinquents--Education--United States. | Juvenile
      delinquents--Rehabilitation--United States. | Critical pedagogy--United
      States. | Narrative inquiry (Research method)--United States. | Juvenile
      detention--United States. | Youth--Effect of imprisonment on--United
      States. | School-to-prison pipeline--United States.
   Classification: LCC HV9081 .B33 2023 (print) | LCC HV9081 (ebook) | DDC
      364.360973--dc23/eng/20220902
   LC record available at https://lccn.loc.gov/2022036911
   LC ebook record available at https://lccn.loc.gov/2022036912

This book is dedicated to my family/friends, Anna, every teacher that has influenced me, every student who continues to inspire me, a wonderful group of support who has kept me going when I felt like giving up, and to God. To my family, my mom is a tremendous source of inspiration. She is a woman of few words, but when she speaks, I hold what she tells me with high regard. She speaks in a quiet wisdom that is always direct. She was the first person to tell me that I was intelligent; her and my conversations will always be the memories that I hold closest to my heart. To my sister, brother-in-law, brother, and "brothers from another mother"—Mel, Albert, Ed, Jeff, and Dave—who I can honestly say always have my back. The confidence to say that I know no matter what the situation, even if I am wrong, they will support me; but be able to let me know the truth face-to-face is a confidence that was absolutely necessary in this long process called life. Your love and support are so valuable to me that the image of you all in my mind brings happiness to the very core of my heart. To Anna, my muse, your confidence in me and pride you show me is overwhelming. The calmness I feel when I am with you allows me to be myself. I had never felt calmness before I met you; your love and ability to get me to relax is overwhelmingly appreciated. I cannot begin to tell you how much I cherish your love and support in this whole process. To my children: Takoda and Azalea; it was you two that inspired me to do this. For Takoda, the way you look at the world is amazing. You have such a unique perspective of the world, and you are truly blessed by God to be able to communicate to the world through your wonderful music. It was a major motivation to pursue reflective arts as a way to know students and have students let us know their stories. I see the wonderful impact art has in your life, and I think your art needs to be shared with the world. To Azalea, your focus and tunnel vision is truly inspirational. Your gift of quiet observation and motivation combined with patience and natural intelligence has inspired me to keep focused and diligent. The obstacles and tribulations you two have overcome at a young age epitomizes true courage. Last, and most importantly, I dedicate this book to God. Every day, I thank God for the inspiration, persistence, and patience it took to accomplish this dissertation. Without God, this book would have never been written.

Contents

Acknowledgments

There is a long line of people who have helped me with this book, and it is only proper and just that I acknowledge some of the most influential folks in my life. I begin with my mentor, Dr. Anaida Colon-Muniz, who has been the quintessential mentor for me. I thank God every day that you were put in my life. You have shown a care and love for me throughout this process that brings me to tears when I think about it. You accepted me as a person and a scholar; you have shown me what it takes to be a scholar. But more than that, you have shown me how to take the responsibility of being a scholar and a human. Your kindness, your direction, your love, your caring is as inspirational as the sunrise. Your influence will transcend this book, for it will be paid forward. Thank you from every inch and ounce of my heart. Also, I thank Dr. Victoria Carty tremendously. Your passion to work with the under-served and marginal populations inspires me to continue my life's work, knowing that we are out there attempting to give voice for those who think their voice is mute. Last, I want to thank Dr. Peter McLaren. Peter's fight is my fight. Peter's experience and direction, as well as our conversations that guided me toward how to direct my fight, have made sure I was not attempting to lead this revolution in education in vain. Thank you Drs. Colon-Muniz, McLaren, and Carty for understanding my passion and challenges, but more so, thank you for being the foundational, steady academic platform that I now stand on. There are not enough words to thank you three enough!

Also, I want to thank every student and every teacher I have ever worked with along my educational journey. You all are probably some of the most courageous people I know. The incarcerated and formerly students who took a chance on me to guide them in academia are amazing. Your trust that I would do the right thing for you all cannot be commended enough. Similarly, the teachers/professors who spend time with your students. Your willingness to educate our forgotten youth makes you heroes because you inspire heroic actions. Any success of this book is largely due to all of you. And I need to

thank the high school and probation staff at juvenile hall who allowed me
to enter their space and supported my attempts and crazy ideas. Thank you
to everyone.

Introduction

This book is written to demonstrate the need for a major change in the alternative and correctional education paradigm. Having over twenty-five years of experience working in correctional education has taught me several important lessons about pedagogy. More importantly, it has shown me how to identify, reflect, and change my own biases. When I took a long step back and looked at the efficacy of correctional education, I noticed that there was little to no efficacy. Frequently, students were being prepared for incarceration. Those who found the way out of the cycle of incarceration were few and far between. The bottom line is that something had to change, starting with me. I had to change. I looked at how I was preparing my students, and I found that I had to do one simple task: I needed to listen. I listened to each of my students. I heard their stories of anger, pain, anxiety, and depression. My curriculum extended beyond the books; my curriculum included the students' voice. Our conversations motivated me to continue to explore the absolute need to recognize and value the voice of the voiceless.

The motivation extended beyond personal experiences, leading me to question the effectiveness of the juvenile justice education system that needs extreme scrutiny due to its responsibility for our most vulnerable population. Education and educational support within the boundaries of incarcerated units is not where students should begin learning the scope of the educational system. But it consistently happens for a variety of factors: the school to prison pipeline (STPP), language barriers, and socioeconomics. Each of these factors plays an important part in students' lack of success in traditional schools, and the factors are cumulative. Consequesntly, students are prepared for education only within the boundaries of incarcerated units, and the academic system perpetuates this model. The importance of the positive educational pipeline begins much too late for incarcerated students; even so, this text will show that it is not too late for students to exit the school to prison pipeline and enter the prison to university pipeline. Before we understand how to attack the school to prison pipeline, we must start looking at how experiences outside the educational system affect the educational experience.

Since students who are adjudicated into the incarcerated life have no choice, it is especially at this juncture when the education community needs to understand this special student population and be more critical of the pedagogy that is employed because it purports to "rehabilitate" students so that they can reintegrate into society. In other words, if the students leave the incarcerated facility and educational experience with the same attitude and perception about education, about life, and without hope, then that approach to education has done the students a disservice and should be questioned and improved. Yet, when incarcerated students are given a more progressive form of education, like the one experienced at the university level or more progressive elementary and secondary schools, they will tend to understand that the true nature of education is to be learners and change agents versus pacified students.

The scope of this book, then, looks at the most overlooked factor in education: the outside factors that influence the educational or the incarceration pathway. Every student has a story that leads them to where they end. The incarcerated students, likewise, have their own stories that lead them to where they are. Their stories can show educators revealing information that can be used to center the educational experience on the student rather than on the curriculum. For curriculum means nothing to a "lost" student. This book brings forward a sample of the stories that give revealing, and sometimes disturbing, backgrounds to what led the juvenile to incarceration. It shows the educational community that the stories of the students go beyond the classroom. In other words, this book attempts to humanize the incarcerated students rather than looking at them as a number.

The purpose, then, of this book is to show that our students have a voice; even the students who want to remain voiceless have a voice. We all are humans; we all have a story. It is my hope that by reading this book, one finds that spark to look at every student as a human, even the ones we find it difficult to make a connection with. This book should awaken the reader to understand that relationships are important to everyone.

The content of this book would not have happened if I did not learn how to establish relationships. My first experience occurred working in a security risk unit. We had no books; we had only lined paper and golf pencils. One of my students, "John," changed my entire outlook on education. John stayed quiet for days, just writing. At the end of the week, I looked at John's writing. He was writing deep analyses of *Don Quixote* and *The Tempest*. I began asking him about the novels and bringing other canonized literature for him to read. He would complete a novel a day and write a detailed analysis by the next day. *The Sun Also Rises*, *On the Waterfront*, and *Love in the Time of Cholera* were just a few of the books he read. We would talk during lunch and after school. We spent hours discussing literature. His intelligence went beyond the "18" tattooed on his forehead. John changed my life; apparently, I changed his. John ended up being released when he was 19. He went to the local community college, Cal Poly Pomona, for his Bachelor's and Master's of Science in Engineering (yes, the tattoo was removed). Now, he works for a major aeronautics company and lives a "good life." I learned three important things from my relationship with John:

1. First, I needed to eliminate all my biases about my students. John was intelligent, but I needed to find the "intelligence" in all my students and be the conduit for change in them. I needed to show them that academia is not a privileged endeavor; it is available for everyone.
2. Second, I can be the key person for my students as an example of the benefits of education, mainly because of my relationship with my students on a cultural level. Since I am from the "neighborhood" and know the experience of growing up in the "neighborhood," I can understand their life experiences. But I also know the life of an academic; I can show students that academia is possible for them too. I have to show them, their parents, and their families that we *belong* in the academic world, just like anyone else does in this democracy.
3. Last, the current common application of schooling for our students is all wrong. Correctional education is attempting to educate students by demanding subjugation and reinforcing oppression. The most meaningful educational experience for John and me was during our discussions; thus, we, educators, need to encourage active participation. Our students learn through conversation, discussion, and debate, not rebelliousness and forced silence.

What I learned during this experience changed my whole perspective about my role as an academic and a teacher. It taught me to look at my profession differently, but it also fueled the motivation to engage in the struggle for our incarcerated population to secure educational rights. I know we all have a "John" in our lives, or a "Billy," or a "Randy," or any of the other characters in this text. This book, hopefully, will give us the energy to change ourselves and our educational system.

Chapter One

The Dehumanization of the Marginalized Student

According to the National Center for Education Statistics (2022), more than 49 million students attended public schools in 2021; broken down even further, a little over 15 million students attended grades 9 to 12 in that same year. Interestingly, childrensdefense.org (2022) indicates that in juveniles being justice impacted through the school system hovers around 300,000; nearly 18 percent of the students in the United States. Similarly, aclu.org (2022) reports that nearly 60,000 minors are arrested daily. Needless to say, both data points are a massive number. Two questions present themselves as a result: 1. Is it probable that the educational system is designed to maintain a steady stream from its classroom to the prison system? and 2. Which students are being justice impacted?

Just raising the questions brings forward debate that questions the educational system and racist intentionality, with every side pointing their fingers at each other. No one, though, is point the finger at themselves. In other words, what am *I* doing about this situation? For example, one person subscribes to meritocracy. This person believes that every student has a chance to succeed if they work hard enough at school. Their efforts will be rewarded. This is true to a certain extent; the truth to this belief relies on the fact that school remains a priority for the student and any extenuating circumstances are kept at a distance.

A second person subscribes to systematic racism. For a number of students, this may be true. There is a significant number of students who are identified because of the color of their skin or their "neighborhood" who are channeled to the correctional system based solely on how they look. This would account for the higher proportionate number of juveniles of color who get arrested or referred over to law enforcement. But is the educational system just another variable in a growingly complex and politically controversial topic? If yes, are we addressing the wrong variable?

Last, there is a third argument that is a combination of the above two phi-losophies. We fail to see what is really happening, though. Young lives are at stake that have a significant impact on not just society, but on the individual life. A child's life, if you will. So, the heart of the question is not whether we are deliberately pushing a certain group of students toward prison. If that were true, our educational system can be viewed as barbaric at best. The ques-tion needs to focus on the efficacy of school and the educational system and how we are nurturing those lives in order to prepare our youth.

Answering the first question presented in the opening paragraph becomes more complicated the further we dig into the question. Schools are not the only factor in the pipeline to prison. Schools do not become the primary fac-tor in leading a juvenile to prison; at the same time, a great number of schools do not become the barrier from incarceration. Consequently, schools have become a scapegoat for juvenile incarceration. For example, an educational system that functions well would eliminate any connection between schools and prison. The inverse is true as well. A "high performing" school does not hold the stigma of a "low performing" school. "High performing" schools are often associated with opportunity and as pathways to universities, whereas "low performing" schools are often associated with gangs and pathways to prison. Do certain schools have a higher rate of suspensions, expulsions, and arrests? Yes. But identifying why that is leads us away from the numerical data. Identifying the root cause of suspensions, expulsions, and arrests needs to be a human reflection. In other words, we need to focus on the person rather than the statistics.

To indicate that education is a pipeline infers that there is a direct line from one place to the other. Students are less on the school to prison pipeline and more on the trajectory that funnels them to prison. There is no doubt that the end result of the academic experience for too many of our students of color is prison, but the pathway to prison is not as simple as a direct line, as many would like us to believe. School becomes the last straw in a series of events that funnels our youth to incarceration. The school to prison pipeline is a complex web of vicious-circle roads, leading to incarceration. Roads that are as complex and confusing as the Los Angeles freeway system.

Our students who are unfortunate enough to become familiar with the criminal justice system understand that they did not take one road and end up in prison. They took many roads that chipped away at their love for learning, thirst for knowledge, and respect for social mores; thus, culminating in arrest. Circumstances outside academia play a factor in the sticky web of incarcera-tion. They encounter negative experiences in the community, and those nega-tive experiences become exacerbated within education. Thus, our students cannot distinguish between either institution: criminal or education. In other words, both institutions become the same oppressive, binding mechanism that works to keep the "at-promise" students on an institutional revolving door. Under closer examination, our school to prison pipeline leads students in so many directions, yet through the same basic experience, that rather than a love for learning and academic success, they experience frustration and surrender to the pressure of their neighborhood's and/or peers' influences and the neighborhood mores.

Thus, the purpose of this book is to give a human voice to the all the quantitative data that exists about the school to prison pipeline, "at-promise" students, and alternative/correctional education; all factors that lead the young mind to prison. Then, we—as educators and humans—can give our students the best chance to succeed in academia by understanding the human experience. In fact, school is the most effective disruptor to the school to prison pipeline. Given that, academia needs to focus on disrupting rather than facilitating the school to prison pipeline. The juveniles who I spoke with understood that school is important, but they learned that the pathway to prison is paved with a multitude of factors, including, and not including, academic experiences. Our students, then, fall into a pattern where school becomes the enemy, and they begin to internalize perceptions that have been directed at them by school and society. As one participant put it:

> They [people on the outside] don't get the full story. They get whether they'll see how the media says, "Oh, this guy's a murderer, or this guy's this [meaning a criminal]." Whereas, you don't know how that person was raised, what kinds of choices were made as far as peer pressure or if something has happened [to that person]. I think the only really one way for them [people on the outside] to see is how that [university] has that program going on. Where they could go in and see everything, how we really are, talk with them on-on-one to see what led them. Really, that's what finally determines it . . . it's like that saying, "Don't judge a book by its cover." You see what they put in front of you, but you won't know the full story until you actually read it, get to know that person.

The above quote shows that the student who is riding shotgun on the school to prison pipeline is not some wild juvenile delinquent. In fact, our school to prison pipeline passenger is a confused, astray person who doesn't know which adult is right or which adult has the best intentions for the school to prison pipeline student. Thus, the creation of laws and ineffective disciplinary procedures allows for the educational system to punish students rather than give the students a true intervention propelling them to prison rather than disrupting the projection. Programs like zero tolerance and Improving America's Schools Act gave ways to punish under the guise of discipline. They allowed for the marginal student to get caught in the web of the criminal justice system, a web that gets tighter the more they struggled to free themselves, until they finally resolve to succumb to the pressures and grips that will ultimately be their demise. To borrow a phrase from my Cousin Jim, "Our students have been okey doked."

THE LOVE TO LEARN AND THE HATE OF SCHOOL

The majority of the juveniles who wind up incarcerated did not begin life, nor school, with the intention of being incarcerated. In fact, most of the people who participated in the program said that they "used to love school" or found school a respite from their home life. So, there must be a point when school becomes one of the pieces that propels the juvenile to prison instead of propelling them to higher education or career training. Consequently, school plays an important role in the lives of an impressionable juvenile.

An explanation of the significant role of the school to prison pipeline widens the picture of the human experience of incarcerated juveniles and the role education plays in their lives. But truly *understanding* the role the school to prison pipeline plays within this population can show how to understand and improve the educational and criminal pipeline created by the school to prison pipeline experience. One participant reflects on the role:

> Once I started kindergarten, I felt intimidated and self-conscious about myself. I was always the troublemaker getting picked on by teachers. I never knew what they wanted me to do since I couldn't understand their language. So they assumed I was doing it [causing trouble] deliberately and punished me for it. Since my kindergarten year, I've never liked nor trusted any of my teachers. For example, when my teacher asked me to move seats, and I just sat there confused, they thought I was doing it on purpose. Ever since then, I felt anger towards them for punishing me.

By the time a juvenile enters an incarceration facility, they already understand the purpose of the school to prison pipeline. During one of the first group meetings with the formerly incarcerated juveniles, I thought it would be interesting to begin the conversation by asking, "Who is the biggest oppressor in your life?" Ignorantly, I thought the answers would include the police, my parents, my probation officer, or the man. I was surprised when the unanimous answer was "school." School was the biggest oppressor for them. This was an eye-opening experience. And it changed my whole direction. I knew, then, that I needed to dive deeper into why, how, and where academia became the most oppressive thing in their lives.

Seemingly, they experienced a relatively positive academic experience until around the eighth grade. One person states, "Eight grade was a rough year, missing school and not attending all my classes. Missing was a big deal for me. I would worry on missing the things that they would be going over." This sentiment was consistent with all the individuals until high school where academic truancy and flippancy became more prevalent. School had not been a place of safety nor compassion, for the individuals were experiencing stressors outside of school that directly affected their academic experience. School became "another thing that I had to worry about, so [they] stopped" attending school altogether. But the desire to attend and do well in school was buried in their will to survive. It became a funeral that saw the death to academia and the birth to a life of criminality.

Once the neighborhood influences became prioritized, their love for school was overshadowed by neighborhood influences and consistent negative academic experiences. As a result, a love/hate relationship with education started to exist. Adding to the changing attitude, schools needed to create a safe learning environment (love), but they attempt to create that environment by eliminating students who may have a challenge succeeding in academia (hate). The rise of zero tolerance policies in education led to the creation of the school to prison pipeline.

The pathway to the school to prison pipeline begins with zero tolerance where students are suspended or expelled for violating a subjective code of conduct whose only purpose is to disconnect students from the learning process (Potter, Boggs, & Dunbar, 2017). Zero tolerance policies that are completely subjective have arisen out of an anxiety to create a safe learning environment for a select student population. School districts use these policies on discipline to force students into the criminal justice system and out of the classroom (Elias, 2013). Heitzg (2009) connects the growing pattern of the school to prison pipeline and zero tolerance: "the school to prison pipeline refers to this growing pattern of tracking students out of educational institutions, primarily via 'zero tolerance' policies, and tracking them directly and/ or indirectly into the juvenile and adult criminal justice systems" (p. 1). It is not a surprise that the school to prison pipeline has created a cause-effect relationship between education and discipline that disproportionately focuses on students of color (McGrew, 2016).

School's role in the pathway to prison is important because it is a major contributor to the pathway, especially for our students of color. Although the purpose of this text is to emphasize the human element, there is a significant need to look at some quantitative data to capture the influence and relationship of race and incarceration. It is impossible to disregard how race is reflected in the data for our students caught in the school to prison pipeline. Juveniles of color are arrested at a rate of 267 out of every 100,000 compared to 31 out of 100,000 of Caucasian juveniles (Sawyer, 2020). Race undergirds discipline practices in school settings; thereby, it undergirds the establishment of the school to prison pipeline for students of color. The disparity of punishment for students of color gives way for the race-school discipline and school to prison pipeline relationship.

Similarly, huge inequities exist in our public school system; inequities that are characterized by the imbalance of punishment based racial and socioeconomic lines (Wald & Losen, 2003). Student discipline data show the unbalanced consequential nature of punishment, race, and socioeconomics. Specifically, the number of all relevant disciplinary consequences show there is a gap in punishment. In other words, if a student of color "gets in trouble" in school, the consequences are going to be more severe than for the white students. Further, as the disciplinary consequences increase, the gap between the number of students of color and white students widens. Thus, there are significantly more students of color being referred to "out of school suspensions" and expulsions than white students, culminating in significantly more students of color being incarcerated. Even though students of color represent less than 40 percent of the student population, they represent over 50 percent of all punitive actions, especially those leading to direct contact with law enforcement. So, the quantitative data is very important because it presents the problem easily and understandable in one contextual arena.

The context of the school to prison pipeline shows that children of color stand a greater chance to receive more punitive actions (Tyner, 2017). The cause of students of color being unfairly directed into the school to prison pipeline is the fact that schools with higher concentrations of students of color are scrutinized with more intense surveillance; thus, an increase in school resource officers' effects on the philosophy of managing behavior and increasing the chances of entering the school to prison pipeline by 5 percent (Nance, 2017; Bleakley & Bleakley, 2018). The disproportionality of these trends, masked by laws that use safety as the foundation, strike a concerning tone (Potter, Boggs, & Dunbar, 2017; Wald & Losen, 2003). Students of color, especially students of color with disabilities, over represent participants in the school to prison pipeline, and the students gaining experience in the school to prison pipeline are getting younger every year (Elias, 2013; Heitzeg, 2009). The quantitative data in this area demonstrates convincingly that youth of color are "more likely than their white counterparts to receive exclusionary discipline in the school system and to be referred and prosecuted . . . that directly contributes to their overrepresentation in the justice system" (Nicholson-Crotty, Birchmeier, & Valentine, 2009, p. 1007), but the data leave out two important factors.

First, the quantitative data leave out the human element. For each of the youth who leave school and find themselves in the juvenile justice system, there is a story; there is a significant story that expands the picture of the student who ends up an inmate. Secondly, and more importantly, the quantitative data cannot lead to a real solution to the issue of juvenile incarceration and effectual education. The quantitative data highlights the problem, but it never identifies a solution. Politicians, educators, and the general public can theorize solutions based on the "numbers"; but solutions based on numbers lack efficacy. The solution cannot address the number; the solution needs to address the human. Thus, the human element, the human story, presents itself as a more significant and clearer picture.

CRITICAL PEDAGOGY AND JUVENILE JUSTICE EDUCATION

Critical pedagogy allows for the human elements to be identified and discussed as factors in the lives of students on the school to prison pipeline and/ or the marginalized juvenile. Critical pedagogy identifies the convergence of theory and education and/or educational practices (Kincheloe and Steinburg, 1997), so applying critical pedagogy to the unequal and unfair educational practices directed at incarcerated juveniles seems to be especially relevant. Juvenile justice education needs to be viewed through a critical pedagogy lens, especially now that juvenile justice education is in the midst of a transformation. Historically, educators have viewed the school to prison pipeline as a necessary evil, for example, collective punishment. So, looking at how educational practices continues its oppressiveness encourages one to question the current pedagogical practices that continue to surface, especially with our students of color and marginalized students. Critical pedagogy pursues the distinction between haves and have nots in a continual attempt to create an equal and democratic society (McLaren, 2015), creating a conflict between traditional practices, with its unequal treatment of students of color, and human kindness.

Critical pedagogy and juvenile justice have a connection. Paulo Freire's broader approach to critical pedagogy shows his constructivist epistemology fits in the juvenile justice education perspective. It does not take long into reading his seminal work, *Pedagogy of the Oppressed,* to recognize that his work can be connected to the juvenile justice educational experience, even though that was not his intention. He writes:

> While the problem of humanization has always, from an axiological point of view, been humankind's central problem, it now takes on the character of an inescapable concern. Concern for humanization leads at once to the recognition of dehumanization, not only as an ontological possibility but as a historical reality. And as an individual perceives the extent of dehumanization, he or she may ask if humanization is viable possibility. (1970, p. 43)

Although he did not intentionally write this paragraph about the marginalized juveniles, it is not a far stretch draw the connection between his contextual intention and juvenile justice education.

The "dehumanization" of the marginalized juvenile and perception of the student on the school to prison pipeline leads one to question whether the educational system treats our marginalized students and incarcerated students with any sort of humanization, which I argue that it does not. The "numbers" do not allow for the humanization-dehumanization relationship to be connected. The tradition of an inferior education that undergirds juvenile justice education supports Freire's identification of the incarcerated juvenile's dehumanization as a "reality." By reading the narratives later in the text of the students who are incarcerated, we can identify that these individuals have a contextual understanding of the extent of their dehumanization. Their stories reveal this recognition. Lastly, the answer to his hypothetical, though, of whether "humanization is a viable possibility" is a resounding affirmative.

Freire's perspective on inequality and injustice has worsened (Darder, 2015), especially in juvenile justice education. For years, I have been advocating for changing the current education model for alternative/correctional education by changing the pedagogy used in correctional and reentry secondary education. Each attempt at changing the "status quo" has been stymied until recently. My efforts consistently were greeted with negative attitudes and answers from administrators and teachers. Yet the ability to hear the word "no" in different ways was not considered a negative; it became a doorway— a challenge if you will—to pursuing the answer "yes." In a way, I accepted McLaren's (2015, p. 119) challenge urging

> to connect these theoretical perspectives . . . to your own experiences in the schools . . . to mediate among the theory presented . . . your own personal history that, if it is not already rich in teaching experiences, is most certainly rich in the experiences of being a student.

I felt education's model did not work for the correctional education student; the model explained by Freire, asking the student to regurgitate "learned" material, skewed the cognitive prioritizing of the incarcerated student; our students on the school to prison track are heavily influenced by other factors in their lives. School had become an additional stressor rather than a place of safety. To make matters worse, school suppressed their "voice," making them a silent, oppressed human. In other words, the voice of the incarcerated students has been worse than lost. It has rarely been heard, if at all, and taken away.

By silencing the incarcerated student, the marginalized student begins to understand their place in society. They begin to understand that their value in society is predicated on them feeling there is no value in learning, no value in education. Essentially, by the time our students become incarcerated, they have given up on education and their "voice." This book looks to give voice to the incarcerated student by bringing their stories to light. By giving their voices light, we can begin to prepare the incarcerated student to end the vicious cycle of recidivism. The current educational model does not prepare the incarcerated student to participate in society and all aspects of life (Darder, 2015). So, I reflected on my experiences as a student of color growing up and attending low socioeconomic schools, my own experience with incarceration, and I reflected on my experiences as a "successful" teacher in correctional education to identify the dehumanization of incarcerated juveniles. Although I did not know it was a form of constructivism at the time, I thought it was interesting that Freire's philosophy *was* my philosophy; consequently, the accepted challenge forced me to look at how we can revolutionize juvenile justice education.

Education needs to change its approach with incarcerated juveniles and the marginalized student to include them rather than push them out; education needs to value their voice and begin to establish positive, motivating relationships with the most marginalized students. Interestingly, John Dewey wrote about the most effective approach to education over a hundred years ago and was echoed by Freire almost seventy years later. Freire comments that students become a "container" to be filled contradicts learning; he accuses education as perpetuating a lack of learning (Freire, 1970). This is true. But what if the "container" is closed, locked, and welded shut? What if the students have given up, not only on education but on life, just as equally as education and life has given up on the student? What if there is no "container"? So even using Freire as a theoretical framework only scratches the surface of how truly "lost" our students caught up in the school to prison pipeline are. Traditional education does not benefit the incarcerated student because by the time our students are flying full speed down the school to prison pipeline, education has taken on a whole new meaning.

One of the misconceptions about students on the school to prison pipeline trajectory is their lack of motivation to attend school. In my experience, nothing is further from the truth. My experience with students caught up in the pathway to prison shows that "at promise" students are consistently outsourced to schools that lack the services to be fully beneficial to the "at promise" student. Students who are on the pathway to prison never lost the desire to go to school; school and life has lost the desire to help the student. School and life stopped listening to these students; consequently, the students lost their voice. The definition of outsourcing students in the school to prison pipeline differs from our traditional belief about outsourcing. Outsourcing students is analogous to "passing the buck" within the educational system.

Students who are failing, truant, or undiagnosed disabled go from teacher to teacher and school to school. At this point, everyone is playing the "lemon dance" game, but there is only one ending to this game—nonattendance—and the outsourcing that culminates in prison begins.

Outsourcing education does not improve the experience for our incarcerated students. The "lemon dance" extends into the lives of children that leads students of color and students of low socioeconomic status into juvenile justice education, giving another example to Darder's (2015) observation on the intention of neoliberals. In fact, it stymies learning to the point that the student learns to never learn. It has heightened the oppression (Darder, 2015) of the incarcerated youth. Freire argues that the teacher needs to allow the student to be an active participant in the educational experience through narrative to reveal the dominant structure and decolonization (Darder, 2015). There needs to be a dialogue between the teacher and student. Each person learns from each other. The incarcerated student understands that the education experience becomes a process of humanization and a practice of freedom (Freire, 1970).

Education should challenge the "lemon dance" that keeps the "at promise" student in normal cultural recidivism. It should challenge cultural recidivism by encouraging critical thinking, self-reflection, and questioning by people of color living in the lower socioeconomic strata. Challenging the cultural and social norms allows for children of color living in the lower socioeconomic strata to challenge how society perceives them. Currently, education reinforces a specific type of education and rewards a working-class education (Anyon, 1980). Sadly, maintaining the undergird of capitalism and working-class labor reproduction has not changed. There is an unconscious reinforcement to an unequal rights education, a backlash still percolating from the civil rights movement (McLaren, 2015) and throughout American history. This is a microcosm of the global divide between capitalism and proletarianism; Marx's economic determinism explains the reinforcement of class perpetuating social reproduction and continuing the class and economic divide that exists in America and is passed generationally among people of color and poverty (McLaren, 1998; Bourdieu & Passeron, 1990). In other words, all aspects of society feed the lower SES student into the pathway to prison, not just education.

This unbalanced world depends on the lack of balance. Incarcerated students need to understand the educational experience as it relates to them and social structures. Incarcerated students need to question. Questions are integral to critical thinking and pedagogy. It demystifies the colonization of schools and allows the juvenile justice student to recognize ableism and racism (Darder, 2015; Annamma, Morrison, & Jackson, 2014). Our students have learned that questioning equates with negative behavior and punitive actions incur; "individuals who enter correctional facilities have an extensive history of academic failure" (Risler & O'Rourke, 2009, p. 225). But questioning cultural norms, the foundation of critical pedagogy, gives juvenile justice students the ability to rethink their place in society; thus, recognizing their place and the relationship between them, society, and the differing cultures that influence criminal behavior (Barton, Corteen, Davies, & Hobson, 2010).

Colonized education facilities have purposely pushed out students of color who do not follow the restrictive academic structure (Baltonado, Harris, & Rutherford, 2005), that is, those who question or challenge the system. Students find that questioning shapes thinking and actions most significantly because each person views the world through a different lens. Questioning their place and role in a colonized education allows the student to reidentify their "self" through critical consciousness, beginning a process of transformation that requires them to question their role in society (Cammarota, 2011). It allows them to recognize critically questioning as a positive action, thus improving education and learning. Racial disparities also create a disproportional outcome in the school to prison pipeline that can be connected to achievement gaps guised as disciplinary gaps (Annamma et al., 2014).

Critical pedagogy seeks to understand cultures; more importantly, it looks to reveal hegemony and expose oppressive forces (Crotty, 1998) giving a counternarrative that give unique insight about minorities (Schwartz, 2015). The experiences of incarcerated youth lend itself to the critical lens. It reveals how the education system has been controlled by the dominant white and insured the success of white students by purposefully sending negative, self-demeaning messages to people of color (Vaught, 2013). The adversity of violence and poverty that children of color experience just by being a minority contribute to the education gap and subjects them to a disproportionate amount of discipline (Gregory, Skiba, & Noguera, 2010). School reflects society's perpetuation of minority hating. The unconscious and conscious oppression of minority cultures need to be exposed, so we can continue to move forward to change social beliefs. The change begins with the young people of color understanding their culture positively:

> Once a person realizes his or her efficacy and ability to transform his or her own and others' experiences for the better, he or she grows intellectually and acquires the confidence to handle a variety of challenges, including higher education, community activism, and organizational leadership. (Cammarota, 2011, p. 829)

Children of color are perceived as inferior, and this perception becomes an exercise of racism in education (Vaught, 2013). Higher education, then, become the conduit to social change for our undereducation of incarcerated juveniles.

Higher education gives another prime example of the skewed message being sent to the lower socioeconomic class. Education has a preconceived idea that it must remain in the confines of repression and reflects societal norms (Giroux & Giroux, 2006). There has been a shift in education over the last twenty years that forces college attendance, but this affects the incarcerated juvenile dramatically because college is not an option for them. Yet political and social dogma proposes and encourages attending college at all costs, but the cost of attending higher education for the lower socioeconomic class preserves their lower socioeconomic status. It forces the incarcerated youth to suffer through the strain of capitalism's tight grasp and influence to maintain the guises of culture (McLaren, 2015). The strangling necessity of loans in order to obtain postsecondary degrees has brainwashed an ideology of American society. The accumulation of huge college debt and pressure of attending a university with no prospects of employment disenfranchises the lower SES student (Darder, 2015). It perpetuates the class driven nature of our society by requiring a college degree and requiring massive amounts of debt in order to achieve it. It guarantees that the low socioeconomic students will never get out of debt and remain poor. This belief affects the incarcerated youth more because they are forced to check the box of conviction; society needs to expose the underlying purpose of forced marginalization (McLaren, 2015) through intentional questions on employment and housing applications. It is a tragedy that students "looking to better their welfare" do the exact opposite.

Sadly, a parallel within alternative and correctional education and socioeconomic suppression exists to become a barrier to higher education. Crotty (1998) refers to Freire to make the connection of the "brute factuality" of humanness with the racial disparity of education. Once students enter juvenile court schools, the fact that their chances for academic and economic success decrease immensely because schools' function does not allow released or formerly incarcerated students to return midsemester (Goldkind, 2011). This forces the former incarcerated student who has been released midsemester to lose credits he or she may have earned. More so, the students must jump into the workforce and postpone school because of the unsmooth transition. McLaren (1998) touched on this when he stated that living in poverty is part of our global economy, so actions like the above are necessary. Taken further, living in poverty is necessary for our global economy. The necessity of our economy to maintain the steep divide between the socioeconomic classes is becoming more transparent. Without an education, the prospects of financial and social success are dreary (Goldkind, 2011). This connection between education and critical pedagogy and social constructs show that juvenile justice education students stand little to no chance of upward mobility.

Consequently, there is a very close oppressive link between poverty, race, and juvenile justice education. A young man of color, who lives in poverty, stands a great chance at standing at the intersection of violence, poverty, crime, and incarceration (Abrams & Terry, 2014). A specific connection exists with correctional education and people of color. Young men with a history of incarceration are unlikely to stop their criminal behavior as adults (Abrams & Terry, 2014). Correctional education mirrors the adult correctional system demographically with "ethnic and racial minorities representing over 67 percent of the population of youths in juvenile detention facilities" (Goldkind, 2011, p. 230). Juvenile correction is supposed to attempt to rehabilitate through education, but education's ambiguous and questionable nature maintains the link between incarceration and education.

The academic experience reinforces the social experience of students of color on the school to prison pipeline. The academic experience reinforces identity development; negative experiences preclude more negative experiences and vice versa (McLaren, 1998). Further, schools become prisons. The role of prisons is to control the deviant behaviors of criminals and change the behavior through, arguably abusive, techniques (Foucault, 1977); schools have followed prisons' lead. Anyon (1980) supports the parallels between the roles of prisons and schools when she examines the "working-class" schools. As a result, a connection is made between institutions, for juvenile justice facilities do not differ from adult facilities in its abusive treatment (Friedman, 2003), nor do they differ from academic institutions. The progression, then, is organic from the working-class schools to the juvenile detention facilities to the adult prison.

JUVENILE *JUSTICE?*

Racism and "white supremacy" explicate the importance of critical pedagogy's role in order to fight against the ignorance (Chomsky and Edward, 1988) against incarcerated juveniles. This holds especially true with the perception of criminality. McLaren's (2003) definition of critical pedagogy as the "politics of understanding and action, an act of knowing that attempts to situate everyday life in a larger geo-political context, with the goal of fostering regional collective self-responsibility" (p. 7) stands most appropriate today. Society has fallen into a vacuum where big business pulls the strings, and lower socioeconomic students are the puppets in Geppetto's play. This charade has flowed into education. The direction of education is obscure at best, especially in the area of social educational justice. The more the idea of social educational justice gets introduced, the less clear and meaningful what education actually means by social justice (Hytten and Bettez, 2011).

Education's fragmentation of ethnicity and ethnic studies, in addition to its attempt at creating a reverse racism dogma, clouds the purpose of a social justice education and perpetuates the school to prison pipeline.

The overt existence of white supremacy in the American culture reveals itself when analyzing the number of non-white minors being pipelined into prison. Ledesma and Calderon (2015) identify scholars examining the epistemological and methodological tools and the experiences of underrepresented cultures, highlighting the existence of racism. Data from the Orange County Department of Education (Ed-data.org, 2021) show that 627 out of 706 students were students of color in Orange County's juvenile hall. Unequivocal data show the propensity of an underlying racist culture in education that leads to incarceration, "illuminating that we cannot truly assess, respond, and promote educational research and praxis devoid of the deep and entrenched nature of [w]hite supremacy" (Ledesma and Calderon, 2015, p. 208).

The manifestation of criminalization of people of color is evident in the arrests and incarcerations of juveniles and adults in the United States. As with adults, the overrepresentation of minorities incarcerated shows the disparity among the races; minorities are overwhelmingly accused and convicted of committing a crime. According to the California Sentencing Institute (2016), the felony arrest rate for juveniles is 503 per 100,000 in Orange County and 681 per 100,000 in California. If 80 percent of this number is people of color, this is a clear indication of the racial disparity and the purposeful criminalization of people of color. This places California as the leading incarcerator of minority juveniles in the world. Consequently, students of color in the juvenile justice system experience oppression that takes a dramatic toll on their mental health.

Education has perpetuated whiteness and constant oppression of minority cultures. "bell hooks, in describing black representations of whiteness . . . the attention here is on the people whose bodies, territories, beliefs and values have been travelled through" (hooks as cited in Smith, 1999). The quote by hooks gives an astute observation regarding the infusion of "majority" culture into the territory of the "minority" cultures as "acts of terrorism." The European takeover of North America was an act of terrorism and reminds schoolchildren every day of the genocide by making them pledge allegiance to the people that executed their ancestors. It is a hypocritical, unclear practicality of how social justice bleeds into the educational arena. Incarcerated juveniles feel it more. They must celebrate the system that purposefully locks them up and continues the brutal genocidal act on the indigenous peoples of North America. This is truer now than it was when hooks wrote her observation, but the context is different.

The context that makes this true is the nature of these terrorist acts; in our case, it is the consistent evolutionary methodology of education to purposely change in order to maintain the Anglican education system that was built during colonialism and decolonization. In other words, education's purpose is to maintain the genocidal purpose of its ancestors, satirizing indigenous cultures with a food fair while making indigenous descendants celebrate their forefather's and foremother's demise by making a mission out of sugar cubes. It is a crossroads of civil rights and American confusion (Schwartz, 2015). The overall effect is the loss of voice of the indigenous student vis-à-vis the loss of his or her indigenous voice.

The parallel between juvenile and adult incarceration justifies an inquiry into juvenile arrests. The viscous maelstrom of minority juvenile arrests frequently begins in public, comprehensive school, where the beginning of the criminalization of the minority juvenile begins. But it does not need to be; most minority students who receive harsh disciplines pose little risk to their school and community (Mallett, 2016). The most obvious offender of juvenile discrimination has been the zero tolerance policies in public schools. A greater number of minority students, particularly African American and Latino students, experience suspension and expulsion as a result of zero tolerance (Thompson, 2016). The institutional use of identifying and criminalizing minority youth blatantly screams racism, for institutions symptomatically use shared societal beliefs, practices, and structures (Vaught, 2013) and draw on these views to collectively and purposely project minority children on the school to prison pipeline.

Common questions that are frequently asked include, "How can we get through to these students" or "I have tried everything, and nothing seems to work? They just don't like school." The inverse is true. School likes to give the impression of welcoming and accepting, and it is to a majority of the students. But as the response that "school is the biggest oppressor" reveals is not that they don't like school. School does not like them. School, being the biggest oppressor in their lives, has crushed their academic spirit, leading to the question of what does it take to reignite their academic fire. Rather than looking to reignite their academic fire through reading, writing, and arithmetic that could reinforce their impression of school, we chose to reignite their fire through an artistic approach that complements traditional academia.

Chapter Two

Inside Voices

The inference of asking some to use their "inside voice" is a passive aggressive way of oppressing someone. In other words, it is telling someone, especially the incarcerated and justice impacted student, to "shut up!" Similarly, incarcerated youth have been silenced for decades, including in academia; they have been silenced with passive aggressive methods as explained in the previous chapter. Research literature has ignored the students who have experienced the pathway to prison (Jones, Ferguson, Ramirez, & Owens, 2018). Limiting the voice of the students who have experienced the school to prison pipeline adds to the psychological impressions of dominance and crime and punishment (Irizarry & Raible, 2014). Only a few articles communicate the voice of the incarcerated college student (Annamma, 2016), even fewer attempt to communicate the voice of the incarcerated juvenile experiencing postsecondary education. As the voices of the students emerge, it should motivate educators to question our role and education's role in continuing a blueprint for contributing to Latin@'s negative image.

The role of "the voice" plays an important role because it gives an in-depth view into the experience of the student; therefore, it gives us—the educator and researcher—insight to methods that will be designed to stop the school to prison pipeline. "Telling the stories of [the] incarcerated and formerly incarcerated . . . begins to disrupt and dismantle the stereotypes people have of incarcerated youth and re-educate people on the critical issues that lead a nation to jail its children" (Winn, 2010, p. 315). Contrary to the belief that "the voice" represents a "false objectivity" rejecting the idea that people of color can have a scholarly voice, personal narratives focus on the heartlessness that occurs in prisons and the issues that lead to prison (Sanchez, 2019).

Academia leads people of color to believe that their voice does not play a role in the literature (Sanchez, 2019). On the contrary, accepting the personal narratives develops a sense of cultural consciousness, especially within Latin@s (Mancilla, 2018). For example, Jordan (2018) identifies an imaginary existence where society impresses a negative image, but counters that mislabel during a biographical narrative that shares how the negative image became a lesson to learn. Sanchez (2019) reflects that his own experience allowed him to realize that his journey gave him the belief for the improbable journey through education; additionally, he realized that he received the "tools and frameworks with which to critically observe and write" (p. 1655) about his experience. Irizarry and Raible (2014, p. 432) support Sanchez's observations: "students connect their school experiences with their cumulative interactions" within education. Voice is important.

If voice is important; then, having ways for our most marginalized population to express their voice is equally important. Arts Based Research emerged as an effective tool for the students to express their voice. Arts Based Research and similar methodologies are necessary to combat the years of negative academic experiences. Negative academic experiences undergird the students' experiences, so educators must seek different methodologies in order for the students to start having positive academic experiences. Because attending school in lock-up facilities is mandatory, school—on the inside and outside—has the potential to disrupt the school to prison pipeline.

If school attendance is necessary within lock-up facilities, there are no truancies. Students begin to experience regular, consistent school attendance; as a result, juvenile justice school has the potential to be a positive and influential experience for incarcerated youth (Blomberg et al., 2011). Essentially, it can be the avenue that leads out of prison, but this is only accomplished if students do not have the same experiences in academia that they previously experienced. Arts Based Research and its methodologies stand out as an excellent academic model for incarcerated juveniles. These methodologies bring a new academic experience to incarcerated juveniles and show the students that academia is no longer bound by "traditional" models.

Even though Arts Based Research is a new methodology in research and assessment that does not subscribe to the quantitative or qualitative matter, it does give enough interpretation to do exhaustive qualitative research. The goal of using Arts Based Research is to unlock the ethnographic puzzle that has been giving past researchers' theoretical, inaccurate, and/or incomplete conclusions about juvenile justice education. Also, Arts Based Research produces a rich ethnographic representation of the educational experience by revealing the unconscious with the conscious to give a complete, detailed picture of the individual experience as a whole.

The use of Arts Based Research seeks to incorporate the "voice" of the individuals through artistic representations of their experience. Ideally, the intention is to give the voice of the participant The artistic representations manifested themselves in fictive narratives and poems. The creative work that became the representations of the students' lives, interestingly, showed how life before their disrupted academic experience became a significant factor.

It showed how "life" affects everyone. Interestingly, it showed how "life" became a catapult into incarceration; thus, it opened a voice that came out singing loudly and beautifully through our interviews and my attempt to give them voice. This text will present Fictive Narrative Inquiry and Poetic Inquiry to give voice through the metaphorical pen.

ART AS EXPERIENCE

Art plays an important part in understanding the experiences that shape life and opinions relating to incarcerated juveniles; as a result, Arts Based Research, specifically written creative ethnonarratives and poetry, was chosen to best present the voice. "The concept of using the arts to reach at-risk youth is nothing new. Called art education, art workshops, arts programs, community art or creative arts therapy groups, these programs are as varied as the names used to describe them" (Ezell & Levy, 2003, p. 108). Similarly, it is not new to ask incarcerated students to explore in the creative ethnography realm. Writing poetry and short fiction allows one to understand the unconscious and conscious parts of life. It allows one to put those elements together in order to create some sense of organized spider web that represents their lives, a connection between learning and life. Art can develop complex relationships between the student and the curriculum through creative expression (Gadsen, 2008). Similarly, creative writing creates a space that eliminates the cultural and socioeconomic barriers of juvenile justice education.

Culture and socioeconomic elements play a significant role for incarcerated juveniles. The use of alternative, creative narratives and poetry gives a small glimpse of their lives that can illuminate learning like those glass-like rays that pierce the clouds after a thunderstorm. Alternative methods of instruction and assessment works best for adjudicated youth. "It is clear that youth in JC [juvenile court] schools have unique and significant needs that may require greater . . . alternative curricular paths" (Gagnon, Barber, Loan, & Leone, 2009, p. 675). It allows juvenile justice students to reflect on their culture and incorporate what they know into a reflection of learning. Arts Based Research becomes a representation of life and learning and gives an indication on how educators can understand the life of the incarcerated juvenile student in order to provide better education opportunities and experiences. There is a lack of examples that shows how art success affects incarcerated juveniles, even though it is reported for incarcerated adults (Ezell & Levy, 2003). It is a pathway of opportunity for the students to understand the extent of education and how learning continues after high school.

Understanding the connection between life, art, and learning emerged at the beginning of the twentieth century; this connection changed the perception of instruction and learning. Even though the connection between art and academic success show promise, incorporating art into the curricular program for incarcerated youth rarely happens (Ezell & Levy, 2003). Eisner and his Stanford University students furthered the use of Arts Based Research as a methodology in the early 1990s. This emergence gave way to Tom Barone's approach using narrative storytelling. Eisner and Barone merely expanded on Dewey's observations. Dewey (1934) touches on the use of art as reflection of learning and growth when he comments how the artists and the art exist simultaneously. Using art as a methodology to understand the human experience (Dewey, 1934) and its importance for cultural and social change becomes the primary focus of understanding how the relationship between art and learning can give insight to culture and education. Yet, the connection between Eisner and Dewey's frameworks has not been linked to incarcerated and formerly incarcerated juveniles—until now.

The relationship between education and experience is over two hundred years old. Arts Based Research was present at the emergence of educational theory; additionally, researchers like John Dewey take the use of arts and experience further in educational theory. Art represents life, and life is represented in art. This is especially true when justice impacted students begin to express their voice through their experience. Juvenile justice students possess the capability to show learning as the summative product of life struggle versus the reception of information (Giroux, 2008). Educators and scholars can use art as expression to show incarcerated juveniles that education is a plausible option. As a result, researchers and educators can use their findings to improve curriculum for college bound incarcerated juveniles. Incarcerated juveniles show a significant positive change academically when art is infused in the curriculum (Stinson, 2009). Knowing the significance of John Dewey's influence on art and education allows one to make the connection of the human experience with a cognitive, cultural, and educational experience. Further, art is education. Education is experience, so art reveals itself in a product based on experience (Dewey, 1934). Art—poetry, painting, narratives, etc.—is an assessment to learning.

A closer connection between experience and art exists with incarcerated juveniles. Art has been shown to produce significant positive change in behavior and academic success (Ezell & Levy, 2003). The learning experience and the artistic experience are closely related. The esthetic nature of art includes both definitions: beauty and principles. Education can only use art when human experience reveals itself (Dewey, 1934). Dewey (1934) began connecting art with education when he argued that art reveals itself in our daily lives, and we use the everyday learned experience as pedagogy. Artistic reflection in education gives incarcerated students the ability to revitalize their perception of having academic deficiencies (Leard & Lashua, 2006).

Using the reflection on the education and life experiences of incarcerated juveniles reveals an opportunity to improve pedagogy for the juvenile justice student.

The dimensions of artistic expressions were expanded by Eisner and his students. They introduced the idea that the quality of research and importance of intellectual inquiry can coexist. Inquiry and artistic composition can be constructed to depend on each other (Barone and Eisner, 2012). Understanding the emergence of Arts Based Research and how researchers approach the field allows one to employ Arts Based Research in juvenile incarcerated postsecondary education (JIPSE). For security reasons, "correctional facilities place restrictions on freedom and choice. Arts programs offer opportunities to exercise decision-making and take ownership and responsibility for something" (Ezell & Levy, 2003, p. 109). It allows researchers and educators to experiment and use a variety of approaches to give way to a new learning experience, for experience and art show an internal beauty (Dewey, 1934) in even the most tortured human.

One may argue that the most tortured humans create the most beautiful art; thus, theorizing that long-term incarcerated juveniles, who were tried and sentenced as adults, have the capacity to excel at postsecondary education vis-à-vis using alternative methods of assessment, specifically using artistic representations to demonstrate learning. Students participate in education where they benefit academically and have a transformative experience (Chavez & Soep, 2005). Also, it familiarizes a critical thinking avenue to learning for the students. In other words, the educator is not constricted by specific, traditional restrictions of academic design, but may incorporate a variety of ways into his or her research (Cahnmann-Taylor and Siegesmund, 2008). An educator can explore new avenues and be creative in his or her methodology. A student in JIPSE can create an artistic work concurrently with his or her qualitative studies to produce an intellectual product.

Tensions arise in creating a symbiotic relationship between life, art, and inquiry. An oxymoronic quality emerges when using Arts Based Research (Eisner in Cahnmann-Taylor and Siegesmund, 2008). "Traditional" researchers and educators may find it difficult to accept that one can practice intellectual inquiry using the arts as the basis of the research. Eisner (in Cahnmann-Taylor and Siegesmund, 2008) argues that the purpose of academia was to give students the possibilities to explore beyond the boundaries of traditional research. He goes further to state that it is within academia where a student has the capability to imaginatively explore methodologies, for places of imaginative exploration rarely exist; but exploration of academic possibilities rarely exists for justice impacted student. Eisner's belief dives into all academia; in other words, the same methodology and philosophy should be extended to *all* students. Using this philosophy, students and educators can use artistic reflections to explore the possibilities of reflection and learning.

Being able to explore new methodologies that go beyond traditional methods creates other tensions according to Eisner. The first tension brings forward the irony of creating an artistic work and using it as a basis for educational research (assessment), as opposed to the traditional, standardized assessment. Art is open to interpretation; as a result, the subjectivity of art surfaces despite the intended conclusions the researcher may have. That dilemma is a risk the educator is going to have to undergo when exploring art as a reflection. Using art to understand human experience goes beyond the aesthetic (Dewey, 1934). Art lends itself to academic pursuits by providing an avenue for researchers and students to imaginatively explore (Cahnmann-Taylor and Siegesmund, 2008). Art gives academia a unique, unobstructed perspective into the understanding and application in order to apply data conclusions; thus, art as expressions of life and learning can be used for a high school mathematics classroom as easily as it can be used for literary analysis classroom. In addition, those interpreting the art may not have the educational foundation to understand intentional messages, so the dilemma of art as reflection relies on the intention and understanding.

The desire to produce a work that gives an open and believable understanding to the person is another tension. This purpose of the reflections may become diluted by my overzealous attempt at creating a highly, sometimes overcreative, artistic piece. Consequently, I must be conscious of the artistic work as it relates to the intention. The relationship of the artistic part of the work must be aligned with the inquiry. Students must have some control their own representation of their identity (Dimitriadis & Carlson, 2003). This becomes a difficult process because the small sample may cause a generalization. A few stories, poems, or paintings have the potential to represent the general. The challenge needs to be exact enough with the examples so that the examples illuminate the learning. In doing so, Eisner explains the nature of reasoning and its effects. First, the tension of deductive versus inductive reasoning arises. Art as representation tends to bring forward specific features to inquiry, but the generalizations and insight from the specific inquiry may create the tension between the differing types of reasoning.

Last, the tension between the aesthetic and reality occurs when aesthetic elements emerge within art by the nature of the unconscious being channeled. The artist's inner emotions and thoughts become reality. Interpretations are molded and shaped through language to create something new (Dimitriadis & Carlson, 2003). Traditionalist may argue that the aesthetic influences conclusions. The aesthetic trumps the epistemological purpose of research (Cahnmann-Taylor and Siegesmund, 2008). But the aesthetic is necessary when using art as a reflection to life and learning. Art cannot be separated from reality; isolating art from the human experience is impossible because art is embedded in life, both working together (Dewey, 1934). Using art as a reflection allows for a cognitively multidimensional expression of life and learning, expanding the experience of the justice impacted student to include the educational experience into the "life" experience. It allows for a more accurate form of assessment for JIPSE students to reflect and produce work that shows learning.

Because art as a reflection of experience may create questions, rather than answers, as a result of the product, it begs one to question the purpose of using art as a reflection of the human experience. Some argue that art as reflections needs to produce answers to questions rather than create new questions. Using art as an expression of life and learning shows that creation of questions is equally, if not more, relevant to producing answers. It goes along the line of thinking in a multidimensional line over linear thinking. Questions are necessary, and they must be asked in order for inquiry to be important. Questions form a more significant purpose (Cahnmann-Taylor and Siegesmund, 2008). Cahnmann-Taylor and Siegesmund's (2008) claims parallel Clandinin in that inquiry is a puzzle that must be put together. The creation of the work and the process resulting in a product holds rigorous importance. Art as a reflection of the human experience needs to produce questions as well as answers.

Arts, by its very nature, recognizes that a subjective portrayal of what the researcher wants to create conflict with the objective presumptions of what assessment is supposed to be. Because the final product is a creative piece, experiences influence the work. The influence occurs unconsciously at times when the artist "gets in the moment"; while the influence can be purposeful. This tension between the purposeful nature of scholarly work and controlling the unconscious nature of creativity constantly asks the student and educator to control the tension in order to have the perfect symbiosis of both.

NARRATIVE INQUIRY AS THE HUMAN EXPERIENCE

The inequality of academics for the juvenile justice student is most revealing in the areas of English—English Language Arts conventions, literacy, and writing—and math. Literacy skills and math skills need improvement. According to 2009 statistics, 75 percent of the 150,000 incarcerated students are high school dropouts and lack the literacy skills necessary to be gainfully employed (Risler & O'Rourke); and in 2008, Kohler and Reese indicate 80 percent of incarcerated students in Arkansas are three to five years below grade level in math. Recent data do not show much improvement. According to Houchins, Jolivette, Krezmien, & Baltodano (2008), "These skill deficits are particularly pronounced in the area of reading. When compared to non-delinquent peers, incarcerated students on average are two years behind in reading" (as cited in Foley, 2001, p. 65). This means that "large numbers of juveniles in corrections are marginally literate or illiterate and have experienced school failure and retention" (Leone & Cutting, 2004, p. 261). In fact, in 2007, an assessment of 398 juvenile justice students, ages 14 to 17, who are incarcerated in three different states, produce supporting results. Their mean standard scores are approximately one standard deviation below the mean on Woodcock-Johnson III letter word identification, word attack, and passage comprehension (Houchins et al., 2008, p. 66). Incarcerated students performing below average on standardized testing is not shocking, but the unwilling nature of juvenile justice education to change the end result for the incarcerated student is shocking. Since reading and math deficits have not changed, different forms of schooling may be effective with students who associate school with failure (Jacobi, 2008).

English and math performance can be improved in the correctional facility; there are data identifying improvement in certain areas even though the data show decline in other areas. Allen-DeBoer, Malmgren, and Glass (2006) find there is an increase in words per minute read and a decrease in error rate with one-on-one instruction in a secured setting. A conclusion may be drawn by reinforcing Platt et al.'s (2006) conclusion about programs that combine tutoring with diploma and general educational development tests (GED) are most effective. There needs to be a rethinking of how education is implemented, an implementation that allows for increased motivation and summative results (Jacobi, 2008). Combining both English and math intervention programs facilitate the students' motivation to progress and their sense of mastery; thus, they perform better on standardized tests.

Despite the lower academic performance, academic improvement is a definite possibility through narrative inquiry. One way to bring the interaction between subjective and objective tensions of the justice impacted student and curriculum is to draw connections between art and learning. One may combine experience and narrative to create an ethnographic story that represents an aesthetic rendering (Leavy, 2013) that allows us to gain a better understanding of the life experience of the justice impacted student. Identifying ethnographic stories can be used to develop a culturally relevant pedagogy and assessment. It strengthens literacy and language skills that emphasize cooperation and collaboration (Jacobi, 2008). D. Jean Clandinin's theories and writings explain Narrative Inquiry and its significance to academia. Narrative Inquiry combines the rich nature of lived experience revealed as data and constructs narratives that piece the incoherent elements, creating a story that the reader comprehends (Leavy, 2015) and the author can show learning. Education is essential in rehabilitation and reducing recidivism (Jacobi, 2008).

Narrative Inquiry uses a foundational design. It becomes a more collaborative engagement with the participants (Leavy, 2015). It has emerged as an influential methodology and pedagogical tool for educational researchers (Kim, 2011). Leavy (2015, p. 39) notes four important converging phenomena result from Narrative Inquiry:

1. The relationship from researched to researcher;
2. The move from numbers to words as data;
3. A shift from the general to the particular; and
4. The emergence of new epistemologies

The "converging phenomena" allows one to construct narratives that reflect the importance of personalized data to reflect how life experiences influence artistic representations and learning. In other words, the narratives become an assessment to the student personalizing learning.

The importance of Narrative Inquiry as a curriculum option plays a significant role because the lives of the students are most revealing when the lives are told from the students' perspectives. Clandinin (2013) reveals every individual experience shapes the person. She writes, "We need to inquire into all these kinds of stories, stories that have become intertwined, interwoven into who we are becoming. These stories live in us, in our bodies, as we move and live in the world" (p. 22). Her astute revelation understands the difficult life the justice impacted student has faced; more importantly, Clandinin understands the connection of all the neighborhood stories to reveal the difficulty the student has in education. Using narrative inquiry creates an appealing, imaginative, understandable story (Leavy, 2015); thus, having the ability to show learning.

Satisfying the design of profiling justice impacted students involves inquiry and feedback that produce unique narratives. "Narrative inquiry in education presents teachers' and students' stories in different literary forms" (Kim, 2010, p. 83). The stories reveal important elements to the life of the urban student. The "unpacking" of the lived stories allows the student to relive experiences; as a result, the student and educator learn to be more responsive as the cultural narratives shift the embedded institutional narratives (Clandinin, 2013). Narrative Inquiry reveals itself in several forms of self-reflected learning, including biographical input, creative nonfiction, narrative method, biographical narrative interpretive method, narrative ethnography, fiction-based research, fictional ethnography, identity research and critical theoretical perspectives. In order to give the clearest representation of the stories of the individuals, analysis of how each work represents the self and the voice becomes an important element in understanding the whole picture.

Just inquiring is not enough, though, stories reveal important elements to the life of the individuals. The "unpacking" of the lived stories allows one to be more responsive as the cultural narratives shift the embedded institutional narratives (Clandinin, 2013). Relying on the *minimalist passive interviewing technique* (Leavy, 2015), both parties rely on their mutual respect and rapport to reveal a story with limited interruption and maximum depth. In this case, the students and I gained trustworthiness with each other over time, thus allowing a multisensory revelation (Leavy, 2015) and emotional, revealing narratives to surface.

So, in a way, I wrote a combination of fictive narratives with narrative ethnographies that educated and played an important role by bringing forward particular truths and social meanings that connect a cultural context with an institutional context (Leavy, 2015). The stories are fictional, but they may hold some elements of real-life occurrences. The emotions and thoughts give a reflection to a distorted mirror that gives a different reflection of reality and social life (Dewey, 1934). The biographical piece has two purposes. First, it will help individuals understand positionality. Further, it establishes insider as well as outsider status. Being able to relate to the individuals' lives because I have walked in their shoes—this relationship will be discussed further in this chapter—gives me "insider" status. Insider status surfaces when the researcher identifies with the individuals' lives.

Because I have multiple areas where the students and I have commonalities, there was an almost immediate "insider" status with me and the students. On the surface level, my appearance mirrors many of the people who come from the neighborhood. Specifically, I am dark-skinned, Mexican with a shaved head and tattoos. Additionally, I have a "hood" accent; I talk like I come from a "neighborhood." Last, my insider status holds importance because I was incarcerated; this gave me credibility with the individuals who have similar backgrounds. I know what it means to be a person of color who has been locked up.

In effect, I was an insider and an outsider. An outsider refers to one who enters a group from which the researcher has no internal affiliation. For example, teacher status places an individual with other educational professional status groups; while it consciously furthers the relationship gap between the teachers and the students. In this case, the participant had a comfortability with me because we connected on several levels even though I was also in the teacher status groups. We connected on the cultural—cognitive and unconsciously—level. The connection led to trust, which led to an open dialogue, which allowed us to produce effective, meaningful ethnographies.

Writing narrative ethnographies allowed us to gain trustworthiness (Leavy, 2015) through the inescapability of art (Dewey, 1934).

Although the intention was to have the individuals write their own fictive narratives, the fictive narratives became somewhat of a collaborative work; I had to get to know the individuals through in-depth interviews. Then, I used the interviews as inspiration to develop a fictive narrative that, hopefully, became a representation of their voice. The collaboration was mutual for two reasons. There was a lot of anxiety because the element of trust had to be built with everyone. The anxiety slowly alleviated as the trust was built and relationships/friendships emerged. The trustworthiness that was established between me and the individuals allowed for them to be open and candid. Because the individuals and I had a rapport that focused on the juvenile justice education, the individuals "trusted" me enough to allow for me to write their stories. Because I was able to be an insider and outsider concurrently, I had to make sure I maintained my subjectivity and objectivity concurrently to write revealing, yet informative, fictive narratives and poems.

FICTION BASED RESEARCH'S IMPORTANCE

Fiction based research creates social research by allowing the authors to express themselves freely. It allows for one to express the complexity of life and the details that are revealed vis-à-vis literary devices. The power fiction carries engages the reader and gives a more transformative representation of research (Nayebzadah, 2016). Fictional narratives employ two features. First, it allows the reader to have access to the thoughts and thought process by giving access to *interiority*; second, it allows the reader to make intentional conclusions by filling in gaps that exist in the stories: *interpretive gaps* (Leavy, 2015). Moreover, fiction-based research allows the student and educator to use description and detail as data, while revealing self-disclosure. Fiction based research gives a "factual representation" that gives the unique opportunity for the reader to identify with a work (Leavy, 2013), likewise, with the stories in this text. The stories give a factual representation of the lives of the individuals. Additionally, it gives access to the reader of the "interiority" of the participant. It gives a brief window of how the participants' lives were affected by the experiences of the individuals, creating the "interpretive gaps" by the settings and unconscious experiences of the main characters. This window can give the light to expose experiences that were once silenced; thus, it allows us to reflect on the experience and open the door of opportunity.

Chapter Three

Loss and Surrender

Although fighting for the most forgotten population in education drives my professional life, one of the most important pieces to the puzzle of how we understand where the gap began to divide and how we can bridge the educational disparity gap is by understanding the real stories. This part of the book does just that. I take the theories, theoretical frameworks, and methodologies; and I look to fuse them together, so the narratives speak to us intellectually and emotionally. There is a bit of a warning, though; a couple of these stories are not the easiest to digest because they delve into serious topics. This doesn't mean that they are academically dense because they are not academically dense on the surface. What makes a few of them hard to read is just how *real* they are. They are emotionally dense, and at times, the stories can become so graphic that it is jarring to say the least. But there is one reality that is in the background of each of these stories; the stories reflect young adults who were serving long term sentences for crimes, which means their convictions and their lives were not for the faint of heart. The challenge was to create a fictional narrative that reflected the lives of the individual. The operative term here is "fictional."

Secondly, I made a conscious decision to use the fictional elements to maintain confidentiality. The fictive and poetic reflections are structured to give the reader a glance at the person's life and how those circumstances fit into their lives. In essence, I wanted to showcase the human element. I wanted to show emotion. As I worked through each story, a few themes emerged: family, loss/abandonment, crime, criminality, and mental health. As I molded the stories, the themes took shape, and I started to see how each one of the themes can be seen in every story and poem. Although each story and poem held some elements of all the themes, there were predominant themes that eventually surfaced. As a result, the fictive narratives were able to be grouped together; this led to where the fictive narratives would eventually be placed. The fictive narratives, then, are placed under two thematic umbrellas: 1. Dealing with loss and surrender and 2. Mental health and criminality.

Under loss and surrender, motifs such as abandonment, isolation, and despair uphold the theme. An overwhelming tone of loss led to feelings of abandonment, isolation, and despair that linger in the fictive narratives. The protagonists literally open their hearts, and they give a glimpse into the conscious and unconscious. Therefore, the first three fictive narratives fall under this theme:

1. Loss and Surrender
   a. "14 Hours"
   b. "Apache"
   c. "Viejito"

LOSS AND SURRENDER

Gianni

One of the first students who joined the program became one of the most reflective students in the program. As with most of the students, there was a sense of stoicism to him. His mind was always reflecting on something else; in his case (no pun intended), he was reflecting on his impending trial. He was looking at some serious time: 25 to life being charged as an adult. In short, he was basically looking at a life sentence because his earliest possible release date would happen around his fortieth birthday, so it is understandable to think that his mind was elsewhere.

This brought up serious questions: why would he care about school if he was looking at 25 to life? What possible relevance would school have if he would not taste freedom until he was old enough to be a grandpa? In fact, the contemplation of the relevance of education came up during the interviews quite a bit with most of the students and became the starting point to a lot of our discussions: why does school even matter if you may not be released until your mid-forties? The weight of this question is beyond fathomable for someone who is not in the position of these young men. First, they were confronted with the reality that their lives were in the hands of *adult* court system, a system that had the reputation of locking certain people up and throwing away the key, even though most were between fifteen to seventeen at the time they were arrested and charged. The second reality was that the pursuit of education, at this point, is moot. There really was no relevance to advancing into higher education because the reality was that a college education was just a fantasy. A bachelor's degree does not hold any weight on the inside. Interestingly, this made any pursuit of a higher education that much more impressive. As I dove into the writing process, I began to see that he was reflective and had a deep desire to reconnect with his family and God.

Richie

Similar to Gianni, Richie Dagger is a very introspective person, and I was curious about how his story would evolve as I interviewed him. I heard from another participant that he was a very good illustrator, so I began thinking about a poem for him because poems can create wonderful images. But when we met, his interviews were challenging, which made it difficult to unravel his story; and I was having a hard time beginning the process. We talked about the educational program he participated in and what he thinks his experience can show those that may come after him. As our conversation progressed, he began to disclose his regret for his incarceration and that his time "locked up" was traumatic. But his life is "turning around," and he is "continuing his education and working at a [major delivery]" company. Also, he just got back from his first vacation ever; he went to Disneyworld with his girlfriend.

I suggested he do a drawing, something like a charcoal or pencil sketch; that would be the easiest way for me to begin the process of writing his story. But he wanted me to write a short story because he felt the short story would allow me to give a deeper sense into his transformation. Since he wanted me to do a narrative, I suggested that I would include the experiences we had in our conversation; while using the experience of the college program as the underlying inference throughout the work. I told him that I would use the classroom experiences and content. More than that, I emphasized to him that there are no boundaries in this reflection; I wanted to explore his entire feelings and experience. Specifically, I told him, "But I am going to give you a challenge. If I write a short story or poem reflecting on the academic experience, I need to try to make it about you, about what you felt underneath the learning that allowed the learning to emerge; trying to combine what was going on in your mind with what was going on in your heart." We continued our conversation. He and I continued contact by email to complete his story through several drafts that took about five weeks to complete.

Randy

Throughout the whole process of working with students in juvenile hall, support must come from administration: educational support and correctional support. The same holds true for this work and for Mister Randy, the principal for the school at juvenile hall. Mister Randy was one of the main factors in the success of working with long-term incarcerated students. He would do anything to provide educational opportunities for the students, even though his hands may have been tied several times due to bureaucracy. He had a genuine love for the students, probably because he had spent half of his half dedicated to the students.

He was in his mid-fifties and had been an administrator for the Alternative, Charter, Correctional, Educational School System (ACCESSS) for twenty-five years, and he had been at juvenile hall for the last seventeen years. Randy began working with ACCESS as a paraeducator (teacher's aide) in La Habra. He became a teacher at the same site shortly after. He taught at La Habra for about five years; then, he transferred to Buena Park. He was an independent study teacher in Buena Park for another two years. At this point, he decided to enter administration. He began his tenure in administration as a vice principal in the same region. After a few years in North Orange County, he was transferred to South Orange County, where he was an administrator in the Mission Viejo and San Juan Capistrano areas. In 2002, he was promoted to the principal position at a juvenile hall. He plans on retiring within the next year or two and moving to a quiet place.

The administration in the local juvenile hall high school was highly supportive in the implementation of the program and Mister Randy was seminal in the entire process of working in the hall. I had known *of* Mister Randy and the good work he was doing in juvenile hall, and I would consider us colleagues. But we never worked together directly until the postsecondary program began. Mister Randy made sure to introduce us to probation staff and administration. In addition, he introduced us the high school teachers and made several suggestions that were used in the development of the program. Mister Randy had an abundance of ideas to benefit juvenile justice education, and his interviews revealed a frustration with his immediate administration, for he felt his immediate administrator was hindering certain college preparatory programs that would ultimately become necessary. The introduction of the postsecondary higher education program through an outside source became a welcomed concept, and his enthusiasm encouraged and inspired the program.

Mister Randy and I met three times for interviews and discussions about the program. He was a little hesitant about his "artistic" capabilities, but I assured him that this was not a measure of his artistic talent; in fact, it would be a measure of my "artistic" capabilities as it reflects his real life. It was an attempt to measure the efficacy of the postsecondary program using qualitative research known as Arts Based Research. We met to talk about the artistic reflection, and our talks kept going back to his love for working with the juvenile hall students and finding ways to make the educational opportunities better for the students. Rather than talk about my "artistic reflection" we always talked about educational opportunities for incarcerated students and what the schools, both correctional and comprehensive, could do to improve the disrupt recidivism. Also, our conversations always included examples of specific students who had visited him as adults, and he literally swelled with pride when he had talking about students "who made it" (note: "made it" implies that the student did not return to incarceration).

He liked the idea of working with me to produce a work; he especially liked the idea of me writing the story. As a result, we met where I discussed what he thought about our university program long-term incarcerated juveniles, both the secondary program at juvenile hall and the postsecondary program. That conversation evolved into his reflection on his upcoming retirement, traveling to remote foreign countries with his wife. I drew the conversation back to the program. Once again, one of the main ideas we got from the program was that he really enjoys hearing from former students who have "made it" out of incarceration. He submitted some notes in a series of bullet points; interestingly, the bullet points were quite descriptive. I reviewed the submission. We met again where I asked him his permission to begin the story and gave him a synopsis of what I was thought would make an intriguing story. We met again, and I was prepared to give him my draft of a story; he read it and loved it.

ETHNOGRAPHICAL INPUT

As I became invested in the narratives, the stories began to steer away from the educational aspect of the school to prison pipeline and more to the humanistic influences of the school to prison pipeline. School was secondary as to why the gentlemen were incarcerated. Their personal lives and decisions became just as relevant, sometimes more, in determining the path to incarceration to the gentlemen. This made the narratives that much more relevant to the educational experience. Their input revealed a multitude of conscious and unconscious factors that can be used to deter one from entering the school to prison pipeline.

The importance of biographical and ethnographical input in the narratives surfaces because researchers are "implicitly interwoven into their final representations in many ways" (Leavy, 2015, p. 39), for example, Narrative Inquiry. Narrative Inquiry relies in description of reality; the result of this necessity cannot be done effectively in an objective manner. Therefore, biographical and ethnographical input is completely subjective. We are getting a glimpse into the life of our protagonist. We would not understand that angst between Gianni and Jesus unless we get this narrative from Gianni's perspective:

15 minutes after I woke up my brother called. It was about noon.

-Hey, what's up, Gianni?

-Nothing. What's up with you?

-Just called to wish you a Merry Christmas.

-Well, same to you.

There was a silent pause then I continued, -Hey . . . Who is this?

-Jesus.

I could feel the distrust and anger creep over me, -Well, same to you, anyway.

The small exchange indicates the brothers have not spoken to each other in quite some time. Additionally, when "the distrust and anger" overtakes Gianni's feelings, we understand the cracked relationship between the brothers. Subjectivity is necessary in order to describe Gianni's reality, so we can scratch the surface on maybe understanding him.

Nor would we understand the complexity of Richie's thoughts and feelings if he was not directly involved in telling his story:

Richie turned and saw the same brown city he just left a few hours ago. It is filled with rubbers and piss. The stink from shit alley thickens inside his lungs. There are no birds; there are no trees to see the wind breathe. On his left winds a road of industrialization, no imagination. On his right, a straight row of no civilization.

The description of the city allows the reader to draw the connection between the author, in this case one of the formerly incarcerated individuals, and the influence of the city from which they grew up. Richie is giving the reader an indication of the negative experience the city has had on him and his life. His hometown is far from a single-family home on the tree-lined streets of suburbia. He is from the barrio. Secondly, the reference to the 6-foot indigenous "looking down at him" references his connection and desire to be connected with his indigenous past, but cannot because of his proximity. "Richie" identifies as Mexican, but he made a deeper connection with his ancestry during his incarceration. By having the indigenous person looking down on the main character and telling the main character to "Stop" shows that the author wants to forget about their past—in this case, incarceration—and move forward with their new life after incarceration.

Subjectivity and experience need input while giving descriptions. I coherently "weave experiences" to distribute an accurate reflection of the data (Leavy, 2015) in the narratives. Putting one's experience into a narrative gives an authenticity to the work; the experiences—past, present, and future—naturally surfaces in the artistic representation. Subjective description is given using dialogue and minimal commentary. Gianni's dialogue shows he is angry at the world and his family:

> We hung out at Grandma's for about 2 hours before the kids started to open their presents. I just sat working on my buzz watching about 20 kids cry about how they didn't get what they wanted.
>
> Finally, I had to step in, -Relax kid. You never really get what you want, so you just settle for the best thing you can get.
>
> Everybody stopped what they were doing and looked at me. They all knew it was true, but they really did not want to believe it today. -Fuck 'em. I thought.
>
> -It's true. And you all are afraid to tell them that their life is going to be fucked up. They're never going to get the girl they want, the car they want, or the present they want.

In this case, I am not weaving my experience into this scene. I am weaving Gianni's experience into this scene. This is not to say that I did not picture my grandmother's house on Christmas; I did. Gianni's story reminded me of my grandmother's house. For me, Gianni's story became the story of millions of incarcerated juveniles, including my story.

Lastly, there is a self-reflected element in their input. "Viejito" reveals a number of areas where self-reflection surfaces. Old Man Dios's reflection on his past and current situation humanizes him, but more importantly, there is a self-reflecting tone when he refers to one of his former students. As a result, there is a depth to the character, the author, and the story:

> Walking to the door Viejito stopped in his tracks and looked down at the ground, then, at the torn screen. A memory came back to him and warmed his entire body like the warm Santa Ana Winds warm the body and gently brushes the hair out of the face. A warmer, yellow smile slowly enveloped his face that brought a small chuckle with it and a quiet nod, "Bridget Madscar? Ahhh yes. I know that name. That girl was smarter that she thought. That girl . . . smart girl. That brazen, talkative, foul-mouthed little chola finally grew up?! Good for you, mehija. Let's go, Pepe, so's we can beat the lunch crowd."

Areas like setting, time, death, relationships, aging, and love become prominent in the story to show the protagonists self-reflection. For example, an aging, near retirement administrator begs for titling the story "Viejito"; it shows a deliberate reflection of life and art. Titling the story "Viejito" shows that the age divide clearly exists. It is how the students see him as the administrator in the school—a little old man. At the same time, it is not a term of endearment, especially in the context of an incarcerated facility. If I wanted to have Randy connect with the students, I would have used a term of endearment like "Veterano" or something similar. I reinforce the age divide and racial divide in the story by using the English version of the term as well when "Viejito" is referred to as "Old Man Dios" at the beginning of the letter from Bridget Madscar.

Even though referring to Randy in the English as "Old Man Dios" reinforces the age divide, it also creates the connection between his personal life and the incarcerated education facility and students. It is revealed in the story that Viejito knows that name of the editor. He remembers her as a chola, which means he remembered her as a Mexican girl from a gang, who was incarcerated. More importantly, he remembered her as "smart," "brazen," and "foul-mouthed"; but he quickly follows those adjectives by saying that "she finally grew up." This statement implies that he knew she had the potential to leave the life of crime, and in this case, she did. In our conversations, Randy always left me with the impression that he felt the same way about all of his students. I honestly feel that Mr. Randy believed that if the juvenile justice education system worked to provide appropriate educational programs to benefit the incarcerated student, it would greatly reduce recidivism. As a result, Bridget Madscar becomes a manifestation and representation of how positive academic and supplemental programs can have an overall impact.

NARRATIVE METHOD

Rather than focus strictly on biographical and ethnographic input with the fictive narratives, it is more important to reflect on the method of how the story was produced. Looking at the stories through the narrative method allows for the stories to be analyzed on a sociological and literary level. Although we underwent interviews, the interviews were not the main component of our relationship. Rather, the interviews were seen as a window that allowed me to get a picture of how life shaped actions, specifically how *actual* experiences reflected and consequently perceptions about academia. For example, a way to analyze a narrative, and its importance to learning, is to apply Bakhtin's framework, where the writer uses multiple viewpoints and voices (Leavy, 2015) based on the cultural interpretation of the word. The methodology allows for diverse meanings to be interpreted, thus, giving the reader a foundation of pivotal moments in the lives of the incarcerated student.

Harvey (in Leavy, 2015) recognizes three elements of narrative when he reflected on Bakhtin's framework:

1. Coherence: Coherence indicates communication. This item is important because participants revel their stories differently [during interviews]. Some may tell the story in a linear timeline; while others may tell their stories in fractured segments. It becomes the researcher's responsibility to narrate the stories chronologically or in a way so the reader may comprehend the story.
2. Turning Points: This item represents the time when the researcher recognizes the point when the participant shifts his or her shift in experience.
3. Re-plotting, or re-storying: This item takes place as the participant reframes his or her life experiences by changing the dynamics of the past to the present to the future (Leavy, 2015).

Using Bakhtin's framework as the basis of the narrative method analysis, the artistic reflections can be viewed according to the three elements in the framework: chronology, turning points, and re-plotting. Looking at the stories, the elements of "chronology" and "re-plotting" occur throughout each of the stories; in fact, the two elements parallel each other. In "14 Hours" the chronology is linear, but the chronology goes beyond what is written in the story, indicating a re-plotting element.

The literal chronology in the story is a brief snapshot of the main character's day, but the end when he refers to Christmas being a "long god-damn time ago" indicates that the time between when the narrative occurs and when it is written is lengthy. This allows the reader to make the connection between the story and the participant's experience in juvenile justice education. Conversely, the chronology in "Richie Dagger" is a different type of chronology; this story is a fragmented chronology and changes the dynamics of past, present, and future—elements of re-plotting also. The story begins with the main character overlooking the ocean; then, it aptly transitions to the city life, then abruptly switches back to the first setting. This fragmentation of the chronology shows the distortion of the events that affect those incarcerated. The abrupt disruption to time is indicative to the abruption of time of those incarcerated. Last, chronology is an important element in "Viejito." In this story, the old man's reflections on his past life becomes main elements of the story; each reflection acting as a character and giving the reader a reflective piece of personal history.

The "turning points" that occurred in the stories happen at the end of each story. In "14 Hours" the turning point happens in two areas: when he realizes that his brother is going to leave, and this may be the last time he sees him and when he reflects on the time he spent with his brother. Gianni realizes that there is a fleeting to time; simultaneously, certain points in time are precious. Gianni feels a sense of loss; time is lost and cannot be recovered. The turning point in "Apache" and "Viejito" occurs at the end of the story as well. The turning point in these stories is the when the main character is confronted by their past and told to stop focusing on the past and begin focusing on his future. For example, when the main character is told to "Stop!" by the indigenous ancestor in "Apache," the main character is actually told to focus on what lies in front of him, and his incarceration is an experience in the past. Every incarcerated person I have spoken with, including myself, has had that "turning point."

The motifs of time and family surfaced during the narratives and conversations. For the incarcerated students, time was important, and why shouldn't it be? They are teenagers looking at possible spending the rest of his life behind bars or an aging administrator contemplating life after career. They openly discussed impending sentences; mostly, they were focused on time. So, when I began working on our fictive narratives, I steered the conversation toward significant moments.

FINDING THE "VOICE"

Soon after beginning the program, the purpose of providing a positive higher educational experience included the process of finding and developing their "voice." The motivation stemmed from questioning the efficacy of the juvenile justice education system. Frequently, students participate in education within the boundaries of incarcerated units because they have no choice but to attend school. The importance of a positive educational experience may never happen for students in juvenile justice due to the students unwillingly attending rather than spending time in a 6 by 6 cell. It is at this crux when the education community needs to understand this special student population and be more critical of the pedagogy that is employed because juvenile justice purports to "rehabilitate" students so that they can reintegrate into society. But if the students leave the incarcerated facility and educational experience with the same attitude and perception about education, about life, and without hope; then, that approach to education has done the students a disservice and should be questioned and improved.

The stories in this section exemplify the resurgence of the "voice." The authors took the essence of the purpose of the study and experience and developed rich stories that described past experiences. At the same time, they showed how they let go of their former "life" and are now moving forward with a new "life." The narrative method approach is based on the experience that incarcerated students are given, including a more progressive form of education, like the one experienced at the university level to show that the emergence of voice equates with a rejuvenation for learning. When there is an experience of a university driven education that values voice, incarcerated and formerly incarcerated students will tend to understand that the true nature of education is to be learners and change agents versus pacified students.

PERSONAL NARRATIVES AND THE
SCHOOL TO PRISON PIPELINE

The importance of giving incarcerated students a voice in academia, research, and literature has ignored the students who have experienced the school to prison pipeline (Jones, Ferguson, Ramirez, & Owens, 2018). Limiting the voice of the students who have experienced the school to prison pipeline adds to the psychological impressions of dominance and crime and punishment (Irizarry & Raible, 2014). Only a few articles communicate the voice of the incarcerated college student (Annamma, 2016), even fewer attempt to communicate the voice of the incarcerated juvenile experiencing postsecondary education. As the voices of the students emerge, it should motivate educators to question our role and education's role in juvenile justice education. Consequently, short fictive narratives give useful, important insight to the incarcerated juvenile's experience that can be used to improve the academic experience, thus, improving the students' potential to avoid recidivism.

The role of "the voice" has importance because it gives an in-depth view into the experience of the student; therefore, it gives us—the educator and researcher—the pathway to stopping the school to prison pipeline. "Telling the stories of [the] incarcerated and formerly incarcerated . . . begins to disrupt and dismantle the stereotypes people have of incarcerated youth and re-educate people on the critical issues that lead a nation to jail its children" (Winn, 2010, p. 315). Contrary to the belief that incarcerated people of color can have a scholarly voice vis-à-vis personal experiences, personal narratives focus on the heartlessness that occurs in prisons and the issues that lead to prison (Sanchez, 2019).

Each fictive narrative signifies the recognition of voice. For example, when the Apache told Richie Dagger to "STOP!," the Apache becomes the manifestation of Richie Dagger's past and present. Thus, the Apache becomes "Richie's" voice. Additionally, it was the realization that Richie's past and present are inter-related that allows Richie to acknowledge his mistakes of the past and can begin to move forward. He must recognize his guilt, but at the same time, he has to "STOP" the behaviors that got him incarcerated and "STOP" suppressing his voice. Additionally, the seagull flying over the ocean represents Richie Dagger's voice and mind, which has now become free. Richie felt a freedom that was otherwise stifled in his current situation, a freedom that was reflected in his short story. The emergence of voice is an expansion of critical thought.

Similarly for Gianni in "14 Hours," the recognition of his past and the significance of his experiences that lived in his memories became the reflection of his "voice." Gianni's story gives an honest approach to looking at the significance of the lives and sociocultural importance in the lives of our incarcerated juveniles. It also gives us an idea of how to navigate our education by tapping into the lives of the students and using that as part of our pedagogy, for example, Culturally Responsive Teaching and Funds of Knowledge. The beautiful, yet direct, blending of all these ideas and feelings suggest that the program was having an important impact on everyone's academic perceptions, thereby showing the importance to disrupting the school to prison pipeline.

This last story in this section is an interesting one in the sense of educational opportunities for incarcerated juveniles once they lose their voice as they become ensnared in the school to prison pipeline. While the discussions were happening between me and students, the conversations with the school's administrator and me began to pique my curiosity, especially since he was very passionate. He began giving me suggestions and ideas about how to improve the educational system for the students. He was passionate about improving the program. We came to the realization that his voice was also being crushed. It was at this point when I thought that having the perspective of the school's administrator was an important piece to the disruption of the school to prison pipeline. In its essence, the administrator's perspective became a reflection or had the undergird of the student-inmate experience in the academic program. Since the hope with using an arts-based reflection was to gain a more accurate, more reflective look into the students' changed or unchanged perceptions about school, the school administrator's story shows how voice is silenced on all ends within juvenile justice. But he does find his voice, and it is echoed in the published poem by his former student.

Using the administrator's voice shows that the students' voice needs to be heard, but it also shows that the voice of everyone involved in juvenile justice academia needs to be heard. This led to a closer look at juvenile justice pedagogical frameworks. Two of the major frameworks that were used when we were working with the students were Culturally Relevant Teaching and Funds of Knowledge. We used the frameworks of Culturally Relevant Teaching (Ladson-Billings, 1995) and Funds of Knowledge (Moll, Amanti, Neff, and Gonzalez, 1992) with incarcerated (mostly Latino) students, with the understanding that Culturally Relevant Teaching and Funds of Knowledge gave the best possible direction on how to employ a different educational model within the institution. The program design used the students' cultural wealth and talent to awaken their capabilities to learn, rather than approaching with the dominant society's cultural capital to school for success, for example, an essentialist educational model. Using these frameworks were motivated by the discussions with Mr. Randy; he gave us the cultural and curricular model to best begin the postsecondary academic program at juvenile hall.

Using these frameworks, the school administrator's advice, my experiences, and the "voice" gave us a true understanding of how to approach a new academic model for long-term incarcerated juveniles. As a result, we learned how these group of students learned. The students' unique approach to learning revealed that we must approach our assessments with a similar uniqueness. Thus, we found that finding the voice was a reflection of learning for the students and for every person involved in the fictive narratives. Incarcerated graduates, incarcerated students, and formerly incarcerated students demonstrated their potential when they are given increasing access to academia and effective critical and culturally relevant learning approaches and strategies. Consequently, everyone produced rich, beautiful works that reflected their experiences.

CONCLUSION

The major theme of loss and surrender surfaces in many areas: time, death, relationships, and love. Loss has been the theme throughout the stories in this section. There was loss of family in "14 Hours"; there was loss of love and past in "Apache"; and there is loss throughout "Viejito." The theme of loss appears in the loss of his wife—the love of his life—and the loss of his memory. Viejito loses his wife, and the tone of sadness permeates throughout the text showing the effect that losing his wife had on him. Viejito's flashback to his wife is a double entendre: it indicates a loss of memory, and it shows how love has affected his life. Secondly, the loss of his memory continually resurfaces. By losing his memory, Viejito cannot remember some of the important elements of his life, but he does remember the significant times in his life. So, Bridget Madscar returning to his memory after a significant amount of time shows that he valued his work within the juvenile justice education field. Moreover, Bridget finally growing up and succeeding indicates to the reader that Viejito's work was not in vain; students in the juvenile justice system can succeed.

STORIES OF LOSS AND SURRENDER

14 Hours

Memories defy gravity as they float up to gently brush the tip of the nose and penetrate the darkest memories. They become an oxymoron of beautiful lavender-like aromas surrounded by the dead cacti. That winter day was especially hot, and I could smell the lavender, rosemary, and sage fighting valiantly against the blood and crack-stained air of Downtown Santa Ana. I didn't want to wake up; I wanted to sleep forever.

15 minutes after I woke up my brother called. It was about noon.

-Hey, what's up, Gianni?

-Nothing. What's up with you?

-Just called to wish you a Merry Christmas.

-Well, same to you.

There was a silent pause then I continued, -Hey . . . Who is this?

-Jesus.

I could feel the distrust and anger creep over me, -Well, same to you, anyway.

-What are you doing today? Jesus asked.

I couldn't imagine why the fuck he was asking me that question. -Nothing. Probably writing some poem about how the world is overcrowded with loneliness. Or maybe I'll have a beer or two.

-Ok. Well. I'm over at mom and dad's apartment. Do you think you might want to talk them?

-No. Just tell mom I said Merry Christmas.

-Why don't you tell her? Jesus asked.

I had to think about that question for a while. I didn't have to think about the actual question about why I didn't want to talk to mom or have her talk to her son. I thought about the absurdity of the question. He knew damn well why I couldn't talk to her; he knew I couldn't respect a woman who can be beaten down for years and never fight back. He knew I could never respect anyone who didn't fight back, but he purposely asked me thinking I would tell him. I found it better to just change the conversation, put him on the hot seat, -Can I ask you a question?

-You just did.

-Yeah. Anyway, why are you calling me? Is this holiday so sick that you feel compelled, almost obligated, to call me? Don't get me wrong, though. I appreciate you calling me, but I haven't heard from anybody in I don't know how long. Now you call me. Just when I was coming to grips with being alone, being by myself and not relying on anyone for anything. I almost forgot about your kind of love. I can't recall if anyone called me when I was down, so why call me now?

There was dead air; Jesus never talks or pulls through when you put him on the spot. I had to keep on railing now that I had him on the ropes, -None of you cared when and if I was throwing my life away. Now you call me, and today of all things.

-I was just wondering what you were doing today, and I thought that since I was down in your part of the world that maybe we could hang out?

45 minutes later there was a knock on my door. I knew who it was. I just opened the door; I didn't even look to see who it was. The door swung open.

-Are you ready? He asked.

-Yeah. Let me get my coat.

On my way up the stairs I thought about them. They never could accept me for who I was, and what I wanted to do with my life. I could hear my dad's smoky breath trying to cloud my visions, -It doesn't seem rational. A boy with your kind of smarts should be a lawyer or something. You should try to better yourself. That was his way of asking why. The funny thing is that I could never really answer him; I never thought he loved anything but himself.

Every step up the stairs another reason and another question came to my mind. Their questions pounded in my skull like my foot pounding on the step. What are you going to do? Where are you going to live; you don't know anything, do you? How are you going to live? What kind of fucking idiot are you? Yet, here I am without any need of them, without any want of them. There were bad times. There were times when I plowed through red lights on my bike hoping to get hit because I was too chicken shit to do myself in, times when I shot, smoked and snorted dope hoping to get hit because I was too chicken shit to do myself in. But I pulled through, and now here I am at the top of the stairs, looking down at the very thing that symbolizes my fears. Jesus looking at how I lived, contemplating how I lived, judging how I lived. I knew I had to go and face him if I really wanted to pull through. I wanted to talk to him; I wanted to walk back down the steps.

I yelled, -Where are we going?

About ½ an hour after Jesus picked me up we arrived at a restaurant and ate. In all, it took us about an hour to get on the road. We stopped to pick up a 6 pack before we started on the 5 North. I cracked open one. I downed about ½ of it in one drink. Then the whiskey. The best combination is ½ whiskey, ½ beer; I called it a "Slow yo roll." Jesus cracked his beer, and he took a pull. He denied me on the whiskey. He said that he never touched the stuff; said it brought out the devil in him.

About 10 minutes up the road, when we were just passing Disney, I pulled out my tobacco pouch, -Do you mind if I roll a cigarette?

-No. Go ahead. Are you going to smoke it, too?

-Of course, I answered in a flustered voice.

-Go ahead. I don't care.

I took out my tobacco pouch and started to roll. Straight fingers; stiff so nothing comes out, not even at the ends, trying to keep it all in the roll. Compact and roll; trying to keep everything together. Twist and lick, nothing wasted. Pack to make it last longer. I struck a white tip match. I thought I was like the match. All that needed to get me going was something to rub me the wrong way.

I looked out at the dirty trees on the side of the freeway and I thought that all trees were the same; they try to reach higher than their brothers until one day they figure out they can't go any higher and just die, leaving their soil to their offspring. I saw my soul not unlike the trees, not unlike the red end of the joint. I felt myself rising with the smoke. It felt good.

-You want a hit?

-Sure. You should have told me it was grass.

-You didn't ask . . . You know what Jesus? I don't even know you. We don't even walk in the same shoes.

We toked and the insane feeling came over me. Here on the 5 North with Jesus feeling like I am heading south but going north at 86 m.p.h. I had whiskey and beer, so why the confusion? What was the reason he called me? Today is Christmas but this is nowhere near a movie. They never wanted to see me before. Why today? Cities that smelled like shit reflected off my passenger window. I thought they forgot me now; I know I forgot them in all this time. Now Jesus calls me out of the blue. It must have felt like years since my orphanism.

We turned off the freeway on Eastern Avenue, right in the heart of East L.A. We made a left, then a quick right onto Eastern. I watched the Indians blend with the Mexicans and I felt home. Drunks walked on the sidewalk with their beers in paper sacks, drinking their flesh. I saw Mary's market and remembered all the times Jesus and I ran across the busy street. I saw my uncle Kiko sitting on the porch on the corner of Eastern and Eugene. He was holding his flesh in a paper sack; nothing ever changes. ½ hour into my stone, we pulled up to my Grandma's house. Jesus didn't waste any time.

-I'm going to the market for some beer. Want some? He asked.

-Sure.

We hung out at Grandma's for about 2 hours before the kids started to open their presents. I just sat working on my buzz watching about 20 kids cry about how they didn't get what they wanted.

Finally, I had to step in, -Relax kid. You never really get what you want, so you just settle for the best thing you can get.

Everybody stopped what they were doing and looked at me. They all knew it was true, but they really did not want to believe it today. -Fuck 'em. I thought.

-It's true. And you all are afraid to tell them that their life is going to be fucked up. They're never going to get the girl they want, the car they want, or the present they want.

-Gianni, could you come to the back with me to grab some beer.

On our way back Jesus started doing what I feared he would always do, -What did you do that for?

-It's true. And sooner or later the kid is going to have to learn about truth. I just thought it would be better if he knew sooner.

-Yeah. But show some respect.

-Fuck that. Look fucker, don't start with that preaching shit. Don't even start, Jesus. I don't want to hear that crap.

-Just try, though, huh?

-I'll do my best.

We left after the presents were opened, and I can't say enough that it was not a minute too soon. It took about ½ hour to drive home. I really didn't want the day to end so I asked, -Do you want to go to a movie?

-Not really.

I invited Jesus into my house out of hospitality.

-You know what? I think I've changed my mind about the movie. There is a good one playing at the village. But I can't remember what the name is. It is an Irish flick.

-The Snapper, I replied.

-What time does it start?

-I don't know. Let me find out.

I looked the movie time up: -It starts in 45 minutes.

-What do you want to do until then?

-Drink wine.

After the movie, we stopped at the liquor store to buy some beer before going to my house. We drank another 12 pack and smoked a few cigarettes. Finally, Jesus had to leave. Once again I started the conversation, -Christmas is over.

-It has been for 2 hours.

-Really? Thanks.

-For what?

-Just hanging out.

-No worries.

I saw Jesus leave my house, and inside I cried a little. I was sad he was leaving, but I was glad that I talked to him. I got to know the brother I never had. He always acted like a father and treated me like a son. I always hated him for that. But that day he was just my brother. That felt good. It's summer now, and I haven't heard from him since Christmas. I know Christmas will forever be in my thoughts. It's summer now, and that was Christmas. Yeah, Christmas, but that was a long god damn time ago.

Apache, or Stop! Richie Dagger

Richie Dagger sat on a rock. The cool onshore breeze made his long black hair flow behind him. The warm ocean made Richie think of the lost loves. Everything seems to have gone in the past. All the ancient love stories about how this girl would last longer than the others. That was all gone, too. Looking into the future made him feel different. He forgot what it was like to be himself. But he sat on the rock overlooking the sea, staring blankly over the great vastness of the entity that was no longer for him. He sat alone in the breeze. The birds must have been asleep. Richie reached in his pocket and took out his American Spirit and papers. Rolled one, lit, and took a big hit. He watched the smoke go behind him.

He didn't know how to stop thinking. How to stop thinking that she was the one for him. The ocean looked great, and her heart was just as big. Too bad he could no longer swim in her big heart. A little girl's voice in the back of his head whispered, "What's the matter little boy? Don't be sad. What's wrong little boy? Please don't cry."

Richie heard the voice like it was right behind him, standing there, almost taunting him. He thought that it sounded like she was right behind him, as if the voice was in the past. Richie knew he was alone, though; there were no birds out in the ocean. There was only the voice inside his head. He wanted to get the voice out of his head. It pissed him off; a chorus of mockeries. He felt he needed a change. He got up and turned around to confront this constant reminder of his past.

He turned and saw the same brown city he just left a few hours ago. It is filled with rubbers and piss. The stink from shit alley thickens inside his lungs. There are no birds; there are no trees to see the wind breathe. On his left winds a road of industrialization, no imagination. On his right, a straight row of no civilization. Richie chooses the uncivilized path. He sees the used needle and rubbers from last night's partying. The hookers, junkies and freaks hang out with the trash; some still jonesing on the night of the feast.

The buildings look empty. The bricks wear paint like clothes. Richie walks down the street until he comes to a dead end. A tall building he can never get by stands before him. Richie looks down at the building's feet.

He thinks of the time they moved in together. She comes out of the shower nude. She's small, 5'1," and has a nice chest; the greatest thing about her is that her tits grow bigger every day. She has blonde hair and blue eyes. Her eyes are more than blue; they resemble the colors of the undying love of the Mediterranean. She likes him better when he sits on a rocker. She likes sitting on his lap. She starts rocking along with him, taking the initiative to go fast, then faster, and even faster. Finally, burning out. Just before her climax, her noticeable eyes change from the loving Mediterranean Blue to the killing California Green. She becomes dirty and everything is no longer the same. The drive is gone. Rocking is no longer laughed at when both of them are done. Supper is always cold. Thinking about her, Richie remembers all the things that make her, but he can't exactly remember what she looks like. At the time she was beautiful; now she is just a memory, like trash-can sex.

As he looks at the building, the sight gets worse. People coming all over her. They spray their whiteness all over her beautiful chest. Every time she tries to wipe away the past, there is another person hoping to be famous. They spew their juices into her walls without the humanity of wiping. The paint on her stomach, the broken windows in her chest; they are all raping a whore for bread. No wonder she can't feel anymore; she doesn't want to feel anymore. Richie is glad he saw her before the broken windows. He glad he tasted the innocence, but that is all gone now. The innocence of this dirty girl and the innocence of Richie is clearly gone, like the fading memory of the crystal ocean.

He starts to miss where he comes from. The big buildings, the trash, all making him into a boy looking at shit. As he leaves the uncivilized path, he looks at the skyline, and the sky begins to rain. Sometimes everybody rains.

The sun starts to go down. Orange highlights crawl over the stained belly of all he loves. The poor building never has a chance in such a big city. He hears the high heels of the first hooker behind him. Richie wants to hang out. He wants to stay with the freaks and the whores. He wants to watch them buy their bread. "Hey, little boy, what's the matter? What's wrong little boy? Don't be sad . . . "

Richie turns around and only sees his past . . .

The ocean looked warmer when the sun started to go down. The shifting offshore wind kept him warm in the oncoming night. The serenity of the warm, salty bay at sunset put all the nightmares to rest, giving him a bit a peace. It felt like a poetic form of drunkenness, true poetry without mentioning a word. Quietness lingered with the smoke. People weren't around to offer a hit . . . or a smack . . . or ugly sex. Richie sat and watched the ocean's smooth back. She was clean. The green ocean ran over and through Richie. He was content to be there. Sometimes the rush of the offshore would send Richie's hair flying into his face. Richie wasn't alone anymore; out in the sea, a single pelican glided over her. It worked the smooth wave. It was going wherever the wind and sea took it. It was one beautiful, motionless, monotone, sex vibe. The voice from behind him returned, though, to break the serenity, to break the acceptance of his new place. "What's the matter little boy? Tchtchtchtch, do not be sad . . . "

Richie wanted this voice from his past to leave him alone.

"Everything is going to be o.k. Tchtchtchtch. Do not be sad little boy."

Richie started to get upset again. He got up and turned to tell the hooker to go away, only to see a 6' indigenous man looking down at him. His long, flowing, black hair flew like the bird out in the ocean. Richie stood transfixed by the blackness of his own eyes reflecting from the blackness of the eyes of the indigenous man. Finally, Richie looked down and saw the ground reaching for the feet of the indigenous man, but it was always one or two inches away. Richie kept looking down out of respect.

The Apache took a deep breath and bellowed from within in a deep voice, "STOP!"

Viejito

The old man has always been waiting, like the last note on a sheet of music, waiting for the fingers to glide over it; a feeling of great anticipation, only to be saddened when the final note was struck and he just lingered in the dead air, going nowhere. Time could never be long enough as long as he remained in Santa Ana; Santa Ana would never give him salvation; he had to wait for his kids to move away. His oldest was a great guitarist, and he still is. He plays for many fans throughout the world and calls upon his dad twice a year if Viejito is lucky; his daughter became a veterinarian and married her college sweetheart. They live in Miami. So rather than waiting, several years ago, he woke up from a restful sleep, packed his bags, and left everything he had known for his new life.

He hadn't slept as well as he did the night before he left, but last night was a particular restful sleep. Pepe, the small and quiet black Chihuahua, didn't even bother him when he went out to chase the rats. Viejito sat next to the window, looking at the old man in the reflection of the window. He was staring at this reflection of an old man with envy through the glassy, blue cataract eyes. He kept watching his lips move as if he was trying to have a conversation but could not comprehend. He saw every desperate tear this old man experienced in his short life. And before he knew it, he was asleep in his own thoughts. Thoughts that came with a glass breaking shock as he realized he needed to get his chores done for the day.

"Pepe!" yelled Viejito from his room. "Where are you, boy?"

He spoke to himself slowly. Sleep stuck in his eyes so badly he could barely open them to see if it was raining or sunny outside. In limped a scrawny mutt, ½ Chihuahua ½ poodle, and sat at the yellow feet of the old man.

"Go get me some pan dulce, huh? And bring me back my change this time."

Viejito put a five-dollar note in the dog's collar/pouch, and Pepe limped out of the torn screen, an 18-wheeler mud flap that Pepe called his doggie door.

Viejito's bones cracked as he tried to get up from his cot, "Uhh. Another day in paradise," he muttered to himself as he finally sat up and wiped the sticky sleep from his eyes. "One of these days Vieja I'm going to find us a nice house out in the middle of the country. You know, my uncle found a nice place. We could do it, too. We could save up all the money, then we could spend the rest of our lives sleeping . . . "

He stopped short when he noticed the empty reflection next to him. He took a deep breath and exhaled, "Ayy, dios mio; con permisso, Vieja. I'm sorry I never gave you the kind of love you deserved. I worked too hard. I am so ashamed that I never let you know how much I loved you. There is so much rage when it is too late."

He reached over to a pack of Marlboro reds on the empty egg crate he used for a table, took one out and lit it up. He took another deep breath and slowly exhaled the blue smoke from his soul.

He struggled to his feet, kind of losing balance but having enough of it left to keep himself from falling over, walked over and lit the candles under his wife's picture. Imagination bled with the first day he met her on the beach in Rosarito. She was sunbathing at the river mouth just at the south end of town. He was playing soccer with his buddies from work. After their game, he swam in the cool Pacific.

"Excuse me," she said while her girlfriends giggled behind her, "My friends and I were wondering if you could open a jar of tuna for us?"

"No problem."

At first, he was attracted to Diana, her best friend, but she was spoken for, so he decided to sit and talk to Claudia. They talked for the rest of the day. She was beaten when she got home because she stayed into the night with a man. Rogelio Burton never stopped asking her father if he could talk to his daughter, and Senor Lopez never approved of their love.

On October 28, 1965, the week of Dios de Los Muertos, the couple met at the same spot they met three months earlier. This time Rogelio had a bag of clothes and money; Claudia had her clothes and life in her bag. They held each other's hand as they set off for their life. They started going north, not stopping until they reached . . . Pepe broke old man Dios' sunflower dream when he barked as he dropped the bag of pan dulce at the old man's feet.

"Where is the change, you silly dog?"

Pepe rolled onto his back to make it easier for the old man to grab his three dollars and fifty-three cents. "Aahh, gracias, Pepe. You really are my best friend in the entire world."

Viejito knew that Pepe could leave him anytime, and he almost cried every time Pepe came back. Viejito walked over to the sink, washed his face and armpits. He brushed his brown teeth with the same soap he used to wash everything, and he combed his oily hair. He walked over to the toilet to do his daily "reading," but he realized as soon as he sat down that he had nothing to read. "Pepe! Will you get the paper for me, huh?"

Pepe sighed as he limped out of his bedroom and out his door to the cold front step. The Santa Ana Winds started up that day, so he grabbed the paper and hurried over to the old man. He dropped the paper and hurried out of the bathroom. Viejito yelled after him, "You're a good dog. Your mother would be proud of you."

Pepe did not wait for the old man this day; he was hungry and wanted to begin breakfast as soon as possible. He walked on the cold kitchen floor and waited at the edge of the small table. He became increasingly impatient. A rare bark echoed through the empty apartment causing the light of the candle to flicker.

"Si.Si.Si. You can begin breakfast; you have been a good boy. But don't eat in a hurry. It gives you gas."

The old man finished his "reading" and took a final look in the mirror before breakfast. He decided to grow a beard. He thought that it would be much easier and cheaper than shaving every day. When he walked into the kitchen, he noticed ½ the pan dulce was lying on his plate, and Pepe on the floor chewing on the other ½.

"You are going to take me to the poor house with your appetite, you silly dog." Pepe made every bit of the bread last. He chewed every bite tediously slow, once in a while looking up at the old man to make sure he was eating all of his share. Viejito suddenly stopped eating his pan dulce, "Has the postman come?"

There was no response.

"We'll go look anyhow."

Viejito came back mouthing a letter, "Hey! Hey you stoopid dog. You put down my food. Hhhmmm."

As he was opening a letter that was sent in a fine envelope, the screen door slammed behind him causing the old man to jump. "I've got to fix that someday," he muttered to himself.

Dear Old Man Dios,

We are pleased to inform you that your poem, "Born Free," will be published in our Summer issue. Enclosed you will find a copy of the magazine and a check for $500. Thank you for your interest in our magazine.

Sincerely,

Bridget Madscar, Editor

P.S. Thank you for everything!

"Born Free? Bridget Madscar?" he asked himself. "I wonder which poem it is, Pepe? Which poem is Born Free? Why is that name so familiar, tambien?"

He walked over to his empty coffee can and began pulling out scraps of paper. "Me Linda." "Thunder." "16 Ways to Kill Yourself Unsuccessfully." He rolled through the poems, but never found "Born Free."

"Oh well. At least we still have some dough for a nice meal. What do you say, Pepe? What do you say we have a nice dinner tonight? But first we have to stop at the bank. Let's hurry so we can beat the crowds.

As he was putting on his good shirt, he noticed an open shoebox next to his typer on the dresser. He looked inside and picked up an aged yellow piece of paper with scratches of pencil on it; it was the poem he had long forgotten about: "Born Free." "Hmm," he sighed as he dropped the piece of aged paper and reflected for just one second on his life, a life that was lived to inspire only to be frustrated with every attempt he made to improve his work.

Walking to the door Viejito stopped in his tracks and looked down at the ground, then, at the torn screen. A memory came back to him and warmed his entire body like the warm Santa Ana Winds warm the body and gently brushes the hair out of the face. A warmer, yellow smile slowly enveloped his face that brought a small chuckle with it and a quiet nod, "Bridget Madscar? Ahhh yes. I know that name. That girl was smarter that she thought. That girl . . . smart girl. That brazen, talkative, foul-mouthed little chola finally grew up?! Good for you, mehija. Let's go, Pepe, so's we can beat the lunch crowd."

Chapter Four

Mental Health and Criminality

The second set of themes includes mental health and criminality; the emergence of a relationship between mental health and criminality was not surprising. Mental health's influence on criminality was more revealing. The perception of incarcerated juveniles is that they are delinquents or gang members who are beginning the path to a lifetime of criminality. What surfaces when the individuals begin to explore how their conscious and unconscious overlap shows that there is a strong undergird of untreated, undiagnosed mental health issues the many incarcerated juveniles experience, primarily from untreated or mistreated stress and/or abuse. According to the Office of Juvenile Justice and Delinquency Prevention (2017), diagnosable mental health disorders exist significantly in juvenile detention centers, approximately 66 percent of the juveniles. The individuals in this text, bravely, revealed mental health issues in their interviews and expressed their fears of the mental health issues resurfacing upon release from incarceration.

Mental health surfaced during the interviews, and I attempt to show the mental health angst and anxiety in the fictive narratives. Few people would be surprised about criminality surfacing because the perception of criminality is obvious, for the juveniles are incarcerated. Interestingly, the incarcerated students were beginning to solidify this perception about themselves. One of the incarcerated students was straightforward with his belief about himself; in his interview, he told me directly, "Yeah . . . I'm just a criminal." His—and others who share—mindset reflected their own perception of themselves.

The realistic nature of the incarcerated youth's life remains constant among every student. They have been removed from civic life, their families, their community; and they are continually being reinforced with the branding of inferiority and criminality (Vaught, 2013). It is not surprising that the effects of the interactions with probation, court, and police become a manifestation of their school experience (Irizarry & Raible, 2014). But it is this unique experience that must be brought to the forefront. Knowing this unique daily life can strengthen a teacher's pedagogy even though the incarcerated student tends to become subjugated and lose the ability to comprehend the democratic process (Irizarry & Raible, 2014; González and Moll, 2002).

Their revelations indicated to me their own mental self-awareness, and they genuinely had a fear of how to function upon release. Moreover, their openness with their disability indicates mental health issues affect the human, so the data above is relevant, but the individuals' stories give the data power—emotive power. Three fictive narratives show the theme of mental health and criminality:

1. Mental Health and Criminality
   a. "Get Some"
   b. "Spaceman"
   c. "Casey Began to Stir"

Each fictive narrative can stand on its own. The writings are works that attempt to show where the thematic relationships intertwine within each fictive narrative. This is where the difficulty in writing this book took place, creating the complex challenge of the narratives as representations of human existence. Even though each story can exist on its own, there are prefaces and epilogues that can be easily applied to each story. Knowing the back story of each individual gives the reader an understanding of the erroneous perception we have of our incarcerated juveniles. We are working with young adults who suffer from disabilities; frequently, they suffer from disabilities that go untreated. Consequently, they commit crimes that could have easily been avoided if their disability was treated. The narratives in this section give a scary, honest introduction to the issues that exist in the everyday lives of our most marginalized population.

MENTAL HEALTH AND CRIMINALITY

Get Some

Incarcerated juveniles fall into the mentality of criminality because they are beginning to recognize that society also perceives them as criminals. This is especially true with the younger population falling victim to zero tolerance policies that criminalize students of color far too quickly. Repercussions from criminal perceptions have replaced basic social needs that lead to criminality and inhibits social growth (Nocella II, Parmar, & Stovall, 2018). As a result, students caught up in the school to prison pipeline become conditioned to criminality, and criminal behavior becomes their only avenue of resolution. Consequently, these young people end up incarcerated for criminal actions that could have been avoided. The same holds true for Patrick. His story is not unique. His incarceration was a result of actions he took, whereas someone with a different background may have chosen a different route. One thing to note about this story: This story is fiction; it is not based on actual events. When I asked Patrick about this story, he said he made it up but that the idea of revenge runs "heavy" where he's from.

Edward, the Spaceman

The number of undiagnosed incarcerated juveniles with mental health disorders remains largely unknown, although there have been studies that indicate a significant number of incarcerated juveniles suffer from some sort of mental health disorder. Truthfully, I was a bit ignorant about the relationship between mental health and juvenile justice because I was focused on the education piece. This short-sighted point of view was awakened when I met Edward. In class, Edward was well-behaved and attentive; at the same time, he was quiet and a bit withdrawn. He communicated his thoughts well when he was called upon in class and always smiled when he gave his input. There was little to no indication he had any issues with his mental health when he was incarcerated, but that would change during our meetings after his release.

After his release, he became a stoic, reserved young man who hardly smiled at all. We met a few times. He would relay his impending homelessness to me when we met, and it was very difficult because I—understandably—had developed a friendship with Edward. We went over his current life and his incarcerated life, and he revealed that he preferred to be incarcerated, which leads to the recidivism factor. When I asked him why he would prefer to be incarcerated, he replied, "Because I could get my meds and at least have a place to live." This brought up two excruciating realizations: recently released persons run the risk of not receiving adequate medication after release. And, at times, the benefits of incarceration outweigh freedom; so, there is not a deterrent to criminal behavior. With these factors in mind, I began working on Edward's narrative. Interviewing and writing Edward's story was like a game of Ping-Pong; Edward and I interviewed several days. Then, I would add and delete multiple drafts in order to try to relay his mental health issues within a narrative as effective and caring as possible.

Casey Began To Stir

To me, this short fictive narrative gives an excellent example of the underdeveloped juvenile brain and impulse control of juveniles. Billy's story was written in a matter of a week. His story was one that evoked some trepidation because of the content. His interviews always revolved around wealth and "making it." In fact, there was always a "name drop" in every interview. He always knew someone who was famous. His interviews were intriguing because we would talk about famous people who became incarcerated. He could not understand how someone who had wealth and some fame could ever ruin it. I asked him if he thought "rich people" had mental health issues. He did not think so. His rationale was that "rich people can just afford a psychiatrist."

Additionally, we talked about what it means to be in therapy and the influence of drugs and alcohol on mental instability. He recognized the similarities between his mental health challenges and others' mental health challenges. Billy felt that those with resources had less of a chance to do "bad things" as a result of their mental health. I agreed but asked him to understand that mental health does not recognize socioeconomics. To that point, he agreed. His story is quite disturbing, but it does recognize that mental health issues exist at every socioeconomic level.

Biographical and ethnographical input in the upcoming narratives gives the narratives an important sense of openness because the narratives discuss fragile topics intersected with crimes. A few devices in the short stories reveal the biographical nature of the story but are not as overt as others. For example, the stories "Spaceman" and "Casey Began to Stir" attempt to show the existence of schizophrenia and how the disease can surface within the individual. In "Get Some," there is an element of revenge and how victimization can lead to criminalization.

Although biographical and ethnographical input is an important technique in Narrative Inquiry, the other frameworks play importance in each story. The inverse is equally true. Other frameworks take precedence, or have more obvious revelations, but the input is noticeable in each story. The ethnography in each story gives it a sense of personal and emotional insight. Bringing in the biographical fiction element into the reflections allows for a creative, engaging text, giving researchers (Leavy, 2013) information that can add to social research, but it gives the casual readers a good story as well. In this section, the different types of input reveal and exemplify the need for addressing mental health awareness in juvenile justice.

The psychological dimension of being incarcerated incorporates a plethora of theories behind the reactions that contribute to the life and stress of the incarcerated juvenile. Frequently, incarcerated juveniles experience stressors that differ from nonincarcerated juveniles, affecting the perception of academia and society. Consequently, the importance of appropriate rehabilitation is imperative if higher education is to make a difference. First, the juvenile's brain has not fully developed. An adolescent tends to act with more emotive responses that are guided by their amygdala rather than their frontal cortex, which controls the thought and logic (American Academy of

Child and Adolescent Psychiatry, 2016). This is evident in the reaction and actions taken by Patrick in "Get Some" when he chooses to take revenge on his attackers rather than face the police—who had shown up by the time the attack concluded—and press charges. The latter is the recommended action by societal norms, but the influence of the neighborhood and the emotive response controls his actions.

The American Academy of Child and Adolescent Psychiatry's (2016) website also claims that the influence of drugs and alcohol furthers the effects of emotive responses; in fact, the organization's website claims, "Based on the stage of their brain development, adolescents are more likely to:

- act on impulse
- misread or misinterpret social cues and emotions
- get into accidents of all kinds
- get involved in fights
- engage in dangerous or risky behavior

Adolescents are less likely to:

- think before they act
- pause to consider the consequences of their actions
- change their dangerous or inappropriate behaviors."

Adolescents from neighborhoods influenced by gangs and gang behavior feel more scrutiny and pressure; thus, the above list becomes more relevant. So, when the protagonists in "Get Some" and "Casey Began to Stir" smoke weed and participate in alcohol consumption during the day rather than go to school, they are reinforcing "acting on impulse" and "engaging in dangerous or risky behavior" because that behavior is encouraged. Specifically, Patrick ("Get Some") exhibits the above last three bullet points when he retaliates against his attackers. He is not thinking about his actions and demonstrates life-changing behavior.

Within the life of the incarcerated juvenile, there is a deep-rooted, highly influential social dimension. The incarcerated juvenile experiences either a heavy neighborhood influence, a.k.a. gang life, or the influence of the school to prison pipeline; more frequently than not, the incarcerated juvenile has experienced both. For some, the life of growing up in the neighborhood revolves around the influence of the neighborhood gang. Interestingly, social mores identify "gang neighborhoods" in lower socioeconomic neighborhoods that are predominantly populated by people of color. The socioeconomic and gang relationship can be attributed to these neighborhoods losing the ability to motivate and correct delinquency (Nuño and Katz, 2018), thus, increasing the number of juveniles joining gangs (Mennis and Harris, 2011). Once a youth joins a gang, violent activity and drug related activity increase; once again, increasing his or her chances of becoming incarcerated. Limited financial resources increase the influence of the gang (peer pressure) and increase the likelihood of gang-like behavior (Griffin, Botvin, Scheier, Miller, & Miller, 2000). It begs the questions: If Patrick was not hanging around "his homies," would he have reacted the way he did; if Billy ("Casey Began to Stir") had positive influences, would he have reacted the way he did; how does mental health become one of the cogs in the school to prison pipeline?

The fictive narrative in "Spaceman" brings up a serious question about the school to prison pipeline and zero tolerance. The rise of zero tolerance policies in education led to the creation of the school to prison pipeline. The pathway to the school to prison pipeline begins with zero tolerance where students are suspended or expelled for violating a subjective code of conduct whose only purpose is to disconnect students from the learning process (Potter, Boggs, & Dunbar, 2017). But what if the student suffers from a mental disorder, especially if the disorder is as serious as the one presented by Edward? Zero tolerance policies are frequently associated with disruptive behavior or minor infractions. The parallel between the zero tolerance policies and mental health is rarely explored.

Subjective zero tolerance policies have arisen out of an anxiety to create a safe learning environment. If schools expel students for an undiagnosed mental health disorder, the school districts have effectively used zero tolerance policies on discipline to force students into the criminal justice system and out of the classroom (Elias, 2013). Heitzeg (2009) connects the growing pattern of the school to prison pipeline and zero tolerance: "the school to prison pipeline refers to this growing pattern of tracking students out of educational institutions, primarily via 'zero tolerance' policies, and tracking them directly and/or indirectly into the juvenile and adult criminal justice systems" (p. 1). It is not a surprise that the school to prison pipeline has created a cause-effect relationship between education and discipline (McGrew, 2016).

Edward's ("Spaceman") story brings forward a serious question: how many of our incarcerated students are suffering from an undiagnosed mental condition? Mental disorders are prevalent in the juvenile justice system. A significant number of incarcerated juveniles suffer from a mental disorder: 40–80 percent (Underwood & Washington, 2016). This means that most of those incarcerated juveniles who enter the juvenile justice education system suffer from a mental disorder, and many of those are undiagnosed. Nichols, Parker, and Kruse (2020) indicate that more than two-thirds of the incarcerated juveniles have an undiagnosed mental disorder. In fact, the incarcerated juvenile's "first encounter with the mental health services comes by way of the juvenile justice system" (Zaman in Nichols et al., 2020). Subsequently, there is an epidemic of undiagnosed juveniles who are being arrested and convicted of crimes that could have easily been avoided if the juveniles received any sort of mental health services.

Edward's narrative brings the issue of mental health to the forefront. The Spaceman travels the streets of Santa Ana as someone who is looking for help, not someone looking to commit a crime. Spaceman pleads for help. There is an anguish and angst in the voice of Spaceman as the contradictions of dialogue and life are brought forward. The juxtaposition of the dialogue in bold with the current dialogue indicates that there are two things going on in Spaceman's brain. Two "voices" are surfacing with the story. One voice is the "normal" person who is homeless and trying to survive in a world that admonishes and degrades homeless peoples who suffer from mental health disorders. The second voice is the "abnormal" person who is angry at the treatment toward him, and the treatment "humanity" displays in our everyday lives:

-Tod. Hi, Tod. A little skater shouted as he passed Tod. The skater was on his way to the remains of a skateboarding ditch that ran along the side of the freeway.

-Oh. It's just a skater.

Tod got up and continued his adventure to the store. His thirst began to grow; he took out his bottle and took a hit of water as he crossed the street.

A car came close to Tod. HONK.—Watch it!

Watchit! Me watch it! You watch it! God, I can't believe the people these days! Yeah, you! If you're some character who thinks of yourself as a sublime being I would beat the living shit out of you! HAAAck phew! Take that! I spit at the way you drive! Oh. Big man gonna git out o' his car and kick my ass! How about it? You think you're tuff! I show you tuff! HHHMMPH. How you like a foot in your ass and my shoe in your mouth? How about that for a little dinner, huh? Well, here's the beginning, anyway! Eat this for lunch!

Edward's story brings a powerful sense of realism that also exists in the juvenile justice system. There are millions of children like Edward and/or Spaceman who will never know or understand peacefulness. They will never understand the peacefulness of being safe, even though they have an overwhelming desire to be so—not unlike the Spaceman.

Fear and anxiety, as a result of a mental disability, connects consequential nature of mental health and criminality. Two commonalities exist with all the participants: anxiety and fear. Those two themes run throughout the fictive narratives. Studies show that distress, combined with anxiety and fear, was often experienced by the juvenile prior to the criminal act (Laajasalo & Hakkanen, 2006). The same happens to Billy during his experience with Casey. Casey wants to end things, but her decision is extremely ambivalent. Her ambivalence could be the result of any number of justifiable reasons, and Billy is not willing to see her reasoning as logical because he does suffer from schizophrenic episodes that eventually leads to his crime. Consequently, Billy's behavior exhibits a logical regression predicting a violent crime (Laajasalo & Hakkanen, 2006).

Billy's psychotic, violent act and perception of the Casey's actions is common among juveniles who do commit a violent act. One could argue that the prediction of a criminal act could be made with each of the stories, leading one to inductively reason that a "history of violence . . . among hospital-admitted psychotic adolescents was described as 'a common behavioral manifestation'" (Gosden, Kramp, Gabrielsen, Andersen, & Sestoft, 2005). In Laajasalo and Hakkanen's (2006) study, they found that offenders experienced either hallucinations or delusions 92.8 percent of the time prior to the offense. So, Billy's, and the other protagonists', behavior could have been predicted, yet there is a key variable: knowledge of mental issues or instability. Billy's story reveals a major issue in the juvenile justice system, one that has a dramatic effect on education. Incarcerated students need more than academia to avoid recidivism; they need help in every area of life that nonincarcerated peoples take for granted.

CONCLUSION

It is easy to conclude that Billy's, and others', criminal acts could have been avoided; on the contrary, none of the criminal acts can be avoided if there is no diagnosis of any mental health issue. This is often the case with incarcerated juveniles. The juvenile justice system, then, becomes the institution that must provide diagnosis and services (Underwood & Washington, 2016) for the juveniles after it is too late for incarcerated juveniles. In other words, a significant number of crimes could be avoided if juveniles with mental health issues received the services necessary to avoid criminal reactions to anxiety and fear. This is not the case, though. Undiagnosed juveniles often receive their first diagnosis while incarcerated (Nichols et al., 2020). Crimes could be prevented, and possibly, lives—including the academic experience—could be improved if the incarcerated juveniles found the assistance in a timely manner.

STORIES OF MENTAL HEALTH AND CRIMINALITY

"Get Some"

I walked up to Gary at about 4 o'clock in the afternoon. My eyes were red like wildfires. I had been blazing all morning and afternoon. It was a morning of bong tokes and *Jerry Springer*.

I looked Gary up and down. He had a freezing look. Gary did not know whether to punch my lights out or confess his entire soul to him, so he didn't choose either. Gary squinted at me, half because he was looking into the sun and half because he was sizing him up, -What's your story?

-What do you mean?

-I mean what is your story?

-I don't have a story.

-Where are you from? What brought you here?

-I don't have a story.

Gary felt this must be the most fuckin' boring person ever to live on this brown earth. -Whatta ya mean you don't have a story? Everybody has a story.

-I don't. I'm just kicking it because of the weed.

Gary thought about it for about a second, -You have weed?

-Umm . . . yeah.

-Well, kick down.

-Roll it.

Gary pulled out some papers, took the weed and began to roll a freshie. -Dude. Where did you get the yellow weed?

-Russ.

Gary took the first toke. The smoke rolled up through the vision, making the dirty birds of DT Santa Ana fly and slowly fade like a slowing record. Gary turned to me, -So, what's your story?

- You really want to know?

About a month ago. I woke up tired; it was right before the weekend. Maybe it was a Friday. I was in the bed staring at the ceiling and clouds in my mind.

Pop pop pop pop pop pop

That sound shaped my environment.

I heard the television in the front room. Someone was up all night on crystal playing the same chord over and over on his bass watching Jerry Springer. The women were yelling about fucking this and that; t.v. was so violent, so bad they said. They were trying to stop the pops; some, I heard, lost friends to the violent pops. Most, I thought, were full of shit. Those clueless chicks were blaming everything but themselves. Mostly they had hatred toward the television. The thing they were on, they were trying to control, and they couldn't even control themselves. What a shame that these people can't figure out the -pop- what happened to them. They developed into huge masses of per-turbed hypocrites who can't get their story straight about was or is right and what is wrong. Television and these imbeciles from Beverly Hills acting like they know what goes on, where the streets are littered with war. Imbeciles, I thought, they don't even know the true feeling of being in front of a camera, because when the camera's flash goes off, they will find what life is all about. The feeling. I wondered if we all felt or if any of us felt.

Pop pop pop popoppopopopopopopop.

I remembered laying on the bed slowly falling back asleep, thinking about a song; it was the last thing in my head before closing my eyes for about an hour:

> "I dreamt all yesterday
> how I'd make a man feel with a gun up to his face
> show respect to me
> I don't care what you're thinking
> I'll wipe that thought away
> that is why I pack my .25
> where nobody knows
> right above my boot
> it's the law and with no one there to serve you
> why not be the hero
> why not be your own?" (Porno For Pyros, 1993)

Pop pop pop pop pop pop. When I woke up again, I stood up slowly, like gravity did its best to hold me down. My head pounded with the pain of a tequila hangover. This old man feeling put me into a slow shuffle to the mir-ror, where I cleaned my eyes—although the white crust gripped it claws in me and left little designs of whatever imagination tells me they were—and put on my boxers.

It was too late to go to school; I just stood there looking into the–pop pop pop pop pop pop–future.

Pop.

I knew that school was out of the way, so I thought about the party going on that night. I used to like to go to parties. My friends and I will get drunk off the keg and watch the jocks try to pick up on sleazy, fake blonde sophomores.

That was the real comedy in my world of forgetful tragedy. At the parties, I would like to think I was somewhere else, in the silence of the park or in the serenity of the beach; the emptiness that would fill my mind would be as big as a the ocean. The ocean always brought me back to the serenity; it was always there. Just as the lights of the oil rigs blinking, blinking . . . blinking green, green, green took me into a world that I really wanted to be in, out of the true reality of the barrio-blinking, pop pop pop. Sometimes lovers would come to reproduce another grain of sand. Then the wind would blow and I fly away. Some of us before others; some of us tonight. We are all in this big beach, knowing we are going to get blown away, but too afraid to do anything about it. Pop pop pop goes the green lights on the ocean.

After getting dressed, I went and had some cereal and started flipping through the channels.

Pop pop pop.

-Fucking television man.

On the news, a man gets his head cut off and they can't find the body, a woman gets abducted and has a fetus cut out of their belly—they know who did it, but they can't find the killer; all these cant's. The president waves "hi" to America and everything is okay until the cop gets killed. More of the same talk shows as before. Screaming people cackling like roosters and hens about fucking this and fucking that. Screaming violently at each other; everything is bad, and nothing is good.

Pop

A coyote falls off a cliff; a pan hits him on the head, and when he shakes his head, everything is okay. On that channel, everything is alright somehow. Everything was cool in there; in those animated moments of bliss and anger. Too bad that's not us in those cartoons.

I finished my bowl of cereal and turned off the television. I called my buddy to see what he was doing. He graduated last year, so most of his afternoons were free. He and his girl were going to the mall. I said, -Fuck that.

I hate the mall. I called my other buddy to see what he was doing. He was going to watch The Gift. *I always wanted to see that movie, so that became my plan. Before going, I needed a pack of cigs, so I went to my room and packed my violence, then went to buy some cigs.*

Pop.

The Gift *was a good movie. Actually, I guess it is still a good movie.*

It was getting dark when the movie ended. The streets were on fire that night, and pretty soon the night would fall into darkness. I would fall into a Friday night party darkness.

It seemed as though the whole party was drinking from the keg. The jocks were doing their thing—picking up on sophomore bimboes. I was hanging out with my homies. We were drinking from the keg, too. None of us had smoke. I finished mine during the movie; my one homie never had smoke, but he's the first to hit you up for one. As I was bumming a smoke from one of the locals, I saw her. She knew I was looking at her, too. I went back to my clique. Just before I reached my friends, she came up to me.

-Hi. I'm Tony, I said. I never give my real name the first time I meet someone; I am not sure why. I just don't.

-Hi. I'm Epiphany.

The rest of the conversation went something like blah blah blah pop pop pop. We talked for an hour, and then the alcohol really started to kick in.

She was giving me sex stares and rubbing on my arm and putting herself on me during the whole conversation, -Would you like to go up to my room?

-This is your house? I was really surprised and relieved by her forwardness.

-Yeah.

-Sure.

I thought this must be my lucky night. It was a long time since I had been with a woman, and that night would not be a moment too soon.

In the room, I put my violence down. It was in my backpack with the rest of the goods. We started making out, and she made the first move, which helped ease a lot of the tension off me. The smooching got hotter and to cool ourselves, we began to take off our clothes. There was something new in her kiss, something that took me from this world and give it all to her. It was the same way I feel when I hold flowers to the ocean. I closed my eyes and saw my back being decorated; I could not leave myself alone; I felt so small, so in control. I opened my wings to fly into her rhythm. Our tongues felt so hard, I knew I would not be able to taste. We went for it.

We started fucking hard. She was on top and working me with the rhythmic motions of the smooth sax player in the coolest jazz band. I was amazed and totally turned on when she turned me over and started kissing my back. When she started tying my hands with her panty hose to bedposts, I was afraid that I might like it. The classical music waved in my head; Mozart began playing "Serenade to the Winds" and those same winds carried me off. I was prepared to be taken by those winds to nirvana. To reach enlightenment in my consciousness with sexual arousal at its highest made the experience into a symphony. The acme of sex is to be carried away, floating aimlessly in the wall of this world, like a cloud. There was a click of a door. I tried turning around to yell at that stupid mother fucker to leave us alone; can't he see we were busy, but my hands and feet were tied to the posts. -Shit, I thought.

I tried looking out of the corners of my eyes. Nobody. I turned my head the other way to find my Epiphany. I did a double take when I saw a big, John Holmes looking dude dressed in a Batman suit.

-Fuck shit! I thought.

He had it all down; he had the black boots, the mask, and the cape. The gray shirt with the emblem on it was just a t-shirt. The only thing missing on the suit was the crotch. I looked around for my Epiphany. She was sitting on a chair by the door smoking a cig. I wanted to be the cig. The very nature of my addiction. The addiction of millions. I wanted to be in her mouth; I wanted to be the smoke getting smoked, disappearing. How can I be the cig getting smoked when I was tied op to a bed with a big—and I mean big—black guy coming at me stroking himself. All I could hear was the stroke of Vaseline hitting twelve.

When he jumped on me, I lost my wind. I felt the plastic costume on my back. The sweaty crotch of my molester was hot and making the plastic stick to me.

I turned to Epiphany and begged her to stop this. She ignored me and slipped the steely dan into herself.

-Please, man, don't do this.

-Relax. You might like it.

Then I felt death inside of me. Screaming its passionate desire to get itself off one last time. It was as if I turned the corner, and I was surprised by a mugger with a gun in his hand; except this guy wasn't a mugger.

-OW! Fucker! OW! Get the fuck off me, fuckhead. Fucker!

The pain was the Grand Canyon without the beauty. I began to sweat. It made it a little easier to take. I felt the skin of his dick. The pain was going away with every thrust. The fair weathered suffering made me blink. I began to think about the consequences of his alive death, -This mutherfucker probably has AIDS.

That was a scary thought that gave the thick smog of his golden teeth swallowing his dirty spit with every line. He kept saying, -Get some. Let's go. Get some. Let's go.

Where can this man have went as he cut through my virginity? He pulled back with spastic thrusts and began to pull me with him. He was going from New York to Los Angeles when his plane crashed. As he pulled and thrusted, the pantyhose that were keeping my hands tied began to loosen. I knew I could slip my hands through the moist tunnel of freedom. I was born again. Epiphany sat on her chair screaming as she was about to get off; she started wild convulsions. I stayed there and took the pain, waiting for it to go away, so I could have my pleasure. His final thrusts positioned his spit like a mauled dog dying young. I felt the bloating of the fucker's cock and was glad that it was over.

As he was wiping his sugar-coated helmet on the sheets, I quietly reached inside my backpack—at least as quickly as I could—and pulled my violence. I untied the other hand and stuck the .38 in the fucker's face.

-Don't you think I at least deserve the courtesy of a reach around? On second thought, get on your knees, Bruce.

He said nothing. He just stared at me with white, scared eyes. The nerve of him to be scared. Jesus Christ, it looked as if this stupid god damned mother fucker was expecting some kind of sympathy.

-And you, my lady Epiphany . . . I think if you can get off by watching that fucker fuck me while I'm down, then, you will really cream your jeans to what you are about to see.

I pointed the .38 at her face and made her get on the chair with the steely dan in her mouth.

Pop. Pop. Two dead perverts.

Pop. Pop. Twice for good measure.

Now they can't go on Jerry and discuss their sexual fantasies.

I walked back to the party. Pop Poppoppoppoppoppop. The band was just finishing its last song. The pit was breaking up; all the moshers were looking for their watches, wallets and whatever they might find in the pit.

My homie came to me; he looked as though he was in quite a hurry, -Hey, man, where ya been? We've been looking all over for ya.

I looked him dead in the eyes, half shut like I just smoked a big fattie, -I was just killing time.

I strapped my backpack on tight; I could smell the gun in my pack.

-We gotta split, man. The cops just rolled up. They're pretty pissed, too. Nobody says they live here.

-We better get the hell outta here, then, huh?

We quickly walked out. I eyed a couple of cops on the way out. We all flowed to the car; the driver was waiting behind the wheel. The door slammed shut behind me and we bailed. Simple as that; simple as turning off the television when the show's over.

"Spaceman"

The wind cried. It made the sound of a child screaming like he had a bad dream, and the cold wind kept blowing. I kept walking. Thunder had a point, but I felt like looking for my way of life; I felt the time was right for me to find whatever the masters of the universe held for me. So, I kept walking. The clouds cleared in the desert sky. I felt I didn't have the right to find myself. I could only apologize for the time spent looking. I kept thinking of her; I kept thinking of Main Street. I take all the blame of the ashes of a burnt downtown desperately seeking attention like a beaten child. It doesn't matter how hard you smack the kid; he keeps coming back for more because he only knows that kind of love. I felt the love pull at my strings; I felt like getting smacked in the head a couple more times. No matter how hard I tried to fight the feeling; no matter how convincing I was to myself, I could not convince myself to ignore the tugging heartstrings. On one side I want to go back; on the other side, I keep yelling to myself, -Hey! Wait! There's nothing there. And the cold sky shimmered and called me deeper. It became darker like a creeping dream, and I was not afraid to walk into the night holes. I felt forever in debt to the night. I kept walking. The dream surrounded me like a stalking Christian:

I stood above the clouds; no, I flew above the clouds following this short bum. He had no hair, and the top of his head was peeling like an ending sunburn. He carried a bleach bottle and an orange trash bag that had "Caltrans" written on the side. He slowly walked past the freeway offramp and down the railroad tracks. I followed him into his home. I flew right above him, and he could never see me. I was his guardian angel.

Tod's space was not very complicated. He did have a mattress, though. There he would sleep, think, eat, and jackoff; all with the worn-out porn mags next to him. He felt the sunlight come though the spaces between the tree branches. This was his favorite part of the day; he could sit and smoke his tobacco pipe. Most importantly, he could talk with the messiah. Tod never took his eyes off the messiah's shoes. The shoes were the shrine. Nothing else. Just Tod, his pipe, his mattress, his mags, and some good conversation.

-There can't be any love in the world. Mmmmm, mmm, mmm. Because there are too many people writing about it. Yeah, yeah, yeah. And these bitches nowadays fuck everybody and fuck everything. They just believe that they can't get hurt, but they don't know that the snake waits for them to fuck, then he can go into her body. It is a feeding cancerous sore on the inside of the body and soul. It puts her into another state of mind. And, and, and then they don't want to fuck anymore. Especially those bitches.

He pointed to the open porn mags by his bed. Tod would rap with the messiah for about an hour, but the smoke was running low. He had to go buy more smoke, so he left the messiah with the knowledge that those little "girl scouts" would be coming soon to do their skateboards and such.

-Bitches!

-Hey! You bitch ass tramps. Someday the trees will overpower those of you who think that you can live without thinking about their future! The summertime will get you in the back. You think you're rich and good looking, then you find yourself crying! Look! Look! See this is what I am talking about! All you inconsiderate right-wing humanitarians think you can rise up one morning with the sun and find everything all right! Am I screaming and nobody hears me? Little do all you know that my wings will take you to the place you fear the most! LISTEN TO ME, MUTHERFUCKAS! Try. Ahhh. FUCK YOU! FUCK YOU! FUCK YOU!

-Fuck you, Spaceman. Get the hell out of my window.

-Spaceman? I thought.—I was sure his name was Tod. Spaceman?

Spaceman stood on the corner of 17th and Main looking at himself in the one-way window just past the fragrant air of tacos and raw meat. He seemed amazed at the tall deep Black face that stared so quizzically looking back to him. The long, brown trench coat in the middle of August didn't help his cause.

Not only could I be right over him, I could read his thoughts, -Man, I hope they come. I can't believe they just left me here. But things aren't so bad here. One may eat easily. But the people are sickening. All the different eyes

trying to watch me. I wish my friends would hurry up. They said, -Once you
are done with your research, then we come back for you. This sun is really
cold. I wish it was hotter. But they haven't come yet. I hope they come soon.

Spaceman looked at the sky. The people driving by did not know what to
think about the man standing on the corner. He looked and looked.

-What the fuck are you looking for; I mean what the fuck are you
looking at! Who do you think you are staring at, me? AAHHH FUCK
YOU! FUCK YOU!

Tod walked out into the sunlight from his humble home. He looked around
at the different scenes. He was living in a place of transition. The old skateboard ditch was no longer there; he laughed, -Yeah, yeah.

The old memories of skateboarders walking by smoking cigarettes and
dope and drinking beer. Kids would walk through his home by the dozens
looking to skate at the Flower Street offramp. The offramp provided the best
ditch skating in Orange County, possibly the Western United States; skaters
came from all over to ride the ditch. There were times when the entire ditch
had kids rolling in and carving with the smoothness and essence of skateboarding. Tod would sit on the bank of the freeway, smoke his pipe and laugh,
-Yeah, yeah.

Now the people of Cal Trans were working in their pumpkin suits to try to
make the freeways look better. -Those bitches. They don't know what they're
doing. Tod laughed at the Cal Trans workers, -Yeah, yeah. I need some eats.

He started walking in the upper middle-class homes of northern Santa Ana;
it was a smooth blend of historical homes with contemporary homes, there
would be Victorian homes next to a brand new cookie cutter house. He was
on his way to the supermarket to buy some more tobacco. Once in a while he
would reach down to pick up a cigarette butt from the gutter.

The skaters would shout at times; they meant no harm. In fact, they revered
"The Spaceman": -Tod. Hey Tod!

-Yeah. You bitches!

Hey, you fucking bitches! Yeah that's right, you! Those muthafucking metal
boxes are killing me! Why can't you lazy asses walk once in a while! Maybe
that is why you are so fat! Maybe you need another hamburger! The bourgeois
eating those laced fat with pickles! And to top it all off, you drive around in
those overpriced metal boxes with the evil fairy on your right shoulder! Hey,
hey; don't look down low at me! Yeah you! Hey! HEY!

-Hey. Hey. Spaceman, you want a B.R.C.?

The spaceman nodded. He loved the beans, rice, and cheese burrito from El
Pollo Loco. He liked the fact that he could finish off one of them with the
change he found in the gutter pleased him. He slowly blinked his eyes, giving him a slight sense of his reality. He tenderly grabbed his burrito from the

counter where it was harshly placed and held it as if he was holding a fallen bird. He turned and walked out of El Pollo Loco and onto Main St.

The usual 5 o'clock traffic bringing its usual participants into the usual scene of tormented domestic boredom bore down Main St. He never understood what the metal containers were all about. He stared at the mixture of smog and oxygen for hours. He was the only one to see the elements combine to form the compound, and it dumbfounded him to an indescribable degree. The frustration burned through his head not unlike the ultraviolet rays burning through his skin. He only wanted to go home, but he was left there to find something. He only wished he knew what he was looking for. There seemed to be nonsense traveling left and right. Up and down. All the sad and angry faces pushing their way into each other. All those people who looked different from him, but they were all looking for a place to go, leaving only the slightest distinction between him and society.

He stopped in front of the pawnshop and looked at himself against the black window. He stood there in a dazed, fixated stare watching the traffic behind him. He looked at his sad face as it merged with the face of the angry drivers.

A small Mexican hipster came out. His greased hair, greased beard, and waxed mustache made him look like everyone else with their fucking tattoos. The irony. -Hey. You! Get away from my window. Hey. Spaceman, get away from my window. Here. Here's a cigarette, man, now go away.

The spaceman threw down the cigarette and cleared his throat.

-Aww, man. Why did you go and do that for? Hey. Hey.

It was not what he was looking for; the basic concept of cigarettes flustered him beyond comparison.

You mindless corrupters of body and soul. Kill me with this. Cough. Cough. Hack ack hack ack. See what you gone and did; goddamnmutherfuckingjesuschristinapopsiclestick, I can't believe you fucksticks. Cancer boys. Hey cancer boys. Hey! Hey!

-Hey. Hey GET AWAY FROM MY WATER HOSE. HEY, YOU FUCKING BUM. GET AWAY.

Tod finished filling up his Clorox bottle and made his way to the supermarket; the whole time, he ignored the man shouting. As he walked further away, the shouts turned into mumbles.

-Jackass, Tod mumbled under his breath as he began walking down the sidewalk toward the store, -Oranges. You need oranges. Oranges are going to keep you going. You really need oranges. Tod climbed the fence into the orange grove to pick some oranges. He stopped suddenly as he heard the rocks crack their knuckles. As he sat listening, he thought it would be nice to sit and talk. A nice conversation, some oranges and a pipe of tobacco makes a man feel like he has a purpose.

-Tod. Hi, Tod. A little skater shouted as he passed Tod. The skater was on his way to the remains of a skateboarding ditch that ran along the side of the freeway.

-Oh. It's just a skater.

Tod got up and continued his adventure to the store. His thirst began to grow; he took out his bottle and took a hit of water as he crossed the street.

A car came close to Tod. HONK. -Watch it!

Watchit! Me watch it! You watch it! God, I can't believe the people these days! Yeah, you! If you're some character who thinks of yourself as a sublime being I would beat the living shit out of you! HAAAck phew! Take that! I spit at the way you drive! Oh. Big man gonna git out o' his car and kick my ass! How about it? You think you're tuff! I show you tuff! HHHMMPH. How you like a foot in your ass and my shoe in your mouth? How about that for a little dinner, huh? Well, here's the beginning, anyway! Eat this for lunch!

The Spaceman walked away from the angry entrepreneur. As he walked, he heard the faint sound of his friends coming to get him. The faint rush of the air beginning to explode in the distance like when the jets of a plane burn through the sky, but you see nothing in the sky. He was excited, but afraid to show it because he did not want his friends to think that he missed them. He stopped on the corner of 17th and Main. He looked up at the sky. As he sat feeling the cool breeze of the sun on his face, a green shoe came down from the sky and hit him on the forehead. He opened his eyes, and he looked at the shoe on the ground. He reached down and picked it up. He looked at the shoe intensely, carefully screening out the possibilities of sabotage and callousness.

He smiled. There was so much happiness. Unlike the filthy sick feeling he got with the cigarette, he wanted the shoe. He wanted to the shoe as badly as every human soul wants true love. He wondered where the other shoe was, and then that one hit him on the forehead. There was the faint sound of "motherfucker" in the distance as he reached down to pick up the other shoe. He smiled again. He knew what he had to do.

He began walking to a construction site. Cal Trans was trying to improve the driving condition for all the vegetarian yuppies of O.C. Spaceman walked right by it; he didn't need a car, so the highway was of no use for him and no longer a distraction. Except it carried the one thing he needed. It was a path for the shoes. Spaceman walked to the construction. He held the shoes so tenderly like he was carrying fragile eggs. He stopped looked up at the August sky for direction.

Tod walked seven steps seven times and looked at the sky to see how much time there was before the sun went down. He noticed the sun was on its way down. He wanted to stop and have a smoke, though, before he went home. He walked behind the Rancher's Market to have a smoke. He sat, packed pipe, and lit up. -MMM_mmmmmm_mmmmmm. Messiah. Where do you think the bitches came from?

He began to talk to the messiah. This time there wasn't any voices coming from anywhere. He began to worry. -Oh no! Where are you!? Have I lost the messiah, and his perfect green feet!? I don't want to be alone! This movie I live in is too ling. We are all disfigured! We are all virgins! Oh no!

Messiah. Shout. He looked up at the sky and began to cry because he thought he was all alone. He did not feel like smoking anymore, so he walked home. His head looking up the entire time.

Spaceman came to the door of Tod's hut. He looked around. He looked inside. He noticed the porn mags, and he paid special attention to the orange trash bags filled with beer cans and soda cans. He inspected them with the attention a Mediterranean artist surveys the sea, looking ever so closely but not touching because he does not want to disturb a perfect scene. He walked over to Tod's bed and set the shoes by Tod's pillow. He looked up for a second, and he had suddenly vanished.

Go on muthas! Take me! Kill meeee! You are all the same! Down there; up here! Gropers, villians, baby killers! Here I am! Everyone's scapegoat! Here I am! Here, cut out my tongue! Here muthas! Creeps! FUCK THIS! I am going to the shower. Hear that! I am going to the shower and piss all over myself!

Tod reached the edge of his home and looked curiously at the sun. It was especially bright at this moment, bright enough to make him squint. The messiah would not and never will answer him. He took a deep breath and a long hit from his bottle. He walked into his home. His eyes became wide, wider than the moon itself when he saw the shoes carefully waiting at the foot of his mattress. He fell to his knees. He remembered the one time he really loved. He slowly reached down and picked up the shoes, held them to his nose, put them down and began to cry. He whispered a scream, "I knew you would never leave me."

"Casey Began to Stir"

The dawn's sun burned Billy's eyes as it crept past the bottom of his windowsill, but he didn't flinch. The harsh rays felt good. Although his eyes remained opened the entire night, he woke with the calling of a new day. This was no ordinary calling. It was not the same as waking up after three days on a binge; it was night, the same as waking after two hours of sleep. He was waking from a sleep that encouraged him the sit straighter. He looked at the clock; it was five o'clock and some change. Casey opened the front door, walked in, and sat heavily next to Billy. He looked into her worldly eyes; he saw the red reflection of his eyes in her gray eyes. Billy's eyes were as red as his heart. He couldn't tell if they were red from lack of sleep or too much booze or both. He thought that it was probably both. He realized that she loved him; she never wanted to leave him, but she had to or she would kill him. She will always come back to him, though, no matter how many times she left the scene. The door would open in the morning. She knew this, and he knew she knew this. Billy stood up and turned so he was standing in front of Casey. He felt big. He reached his hand out and invited her into the bed, so they could take the final turn into the twisted thoughts of everything that encouraged their love and friendship. No apologies; none were needed. She took his hand and followed him to the bed.

They were beautiful people. They had perfect bodies to complement their imperfect minds. They felt they belonged together. There wasn't a better fit. Making love was a sweet song displaying their affections. Billy kissed her neck passionately, not because he wanted to but because he knew it would turn her on. He knew the breathing would begin to rise and her chest would rise with it. The waiting drove her mad. She grabbed his head and pulled it closely to hers. Their sinning began. Her nipples became rock hard, and Billy felt himself fill with enjoyment and misery. The two flowed like sweet harmonica winds blowing through long flowing brown hair. Billy's hair mixed perfectly with Casey's. Casey's love for him grew with every loving, hollow kiss. -I want to fuck you, she whispered into his ears.

Billy turned over, and pulled her on top of him,

-Fuck me. The two strummed through the sex. They followed the rhythm and flow of the cool ocean's waves until they both found home.

The next morning felt like a bad hangover. Sex hadn't killed Billy yet. He looked over to his watch; it stared him down like a desperado waiting to shoot him between the eyes. -Six o' fucking clock. Yeah, this kind of shit is going to snuff me out yet. I ain't dead yet.

Casey began to stir. Billy went to take a leak so he wouldn't disturb her. As he walked back to the bed, half hoping she wasn't there and half-hoping she was still sleeping, he noticed she was sitting up smoking her Camel. She enjoyed the smoke filter through the air and lungs. It was a machine gun rifling through the air. Billy found it difficult to work his way through the smoke to find the enemy, -Hey. Let's go to the beach.

Billy saw the stinging eyes following his every step. He walked over to the radio and flipped it on one of the gross morning shows overplaying the same bits day after day. It made Billy feel like an old man; the limit of airplay squeezed his brain into a small ball. He impatiently turned the dial. Finally, he found a song worth listening,

-*Sweetness. Sweetness, I was only joking when I said I'd like to mash every tooth in your head. Sweetness. Oh ho sweetness, I was only joking.*

Billy turned quietly to Casey, -So who were you on the phone with the other day?

-I thought we finished this conversation.

-I didn't finish this conversation.

She sat there smiling, -You son of a bitch. You can't get enough.

He didn't like the way she was smiling. -Fuck it. I get it. Let's go to the beach.

In the car, the two sat staring at the gray roads below the black tires. A small drizzle perspired on the windshield, and Billy didn't have any wipers, but that didn't stop him from stepping on the gas pedal.

A bit of fear ran down Casey's spine; it was one of the few times she found fear, -Slow down.

Billy smiled at her request and stepped harder on the pedal. The small brown B-210 could only top 55 on a good day, but the slick roads from the first rain made the driving a bit more dangerous than normal. Casey's fear began spreading into her head, -Fred. Please slow down.

Billy's smile grew even wider, -Who's Fred?

Casey's oh shit thought consumed her mind. -He's an old friend who drove like shit. You're reminding me of him right now.

-Hhhmmm.

And Billy kept driving faster. Billy began to turn into a mess because he was letting her get into his head. Casey couldn't handle it anymore, -Look Billy. I don't want to see you anymore and I don't want to die. So please slow down.

Billy let a little loose on the pedal, -What?

-Everything has changed, and nothing has changed. I don't feel we are being one. So, I don't want to see you anymore.

Billy sat in silence for about ten seconds; then, he turned his attention to the road. His only reply was to step on the pedal again and hum. Anything else she had to say, he didn't want to hear. He just thought, -I don't want to lose you; can't you see that this isn't making me happy.

They were getting close to the beach. Billy began to look for a parking spot. -Billy. This relationship isn't making me happy anymore. I think I want to go home. I don't want to be here.

Casey quickly got out of the car. Billy quickly drove after her, -Here. Let me give you a ride home.

-I'm not going home.

-Where are you going?

-I am not sure. I don't really have anywhere to go.

-I'll give you a ride anywhere. I will take you to wherever you want to go.

-Okay. I think I want to go to Stacy's place.

She got back in the car. Billy drove to Stacy's house listening to the very hairy cries shitting into his eyes. Feeling the traveling like some hot heroin caught like Jesus just before he faced the Pilate. He parked in front of Stacy's house and did not even notice that she broke the heel of her shoe until she got out of the car.

-What happened to your shoe?

-It broke when you pushed me out of the car.

-Hhmmph.

Casey turned to Billy, -Will you call me later?

-*Will you call me later!? Maybe a blue pen and a car door just might help me jump your bones. I can't go in. I can't go in on it.* I leave next week for Vegas.

-Call me when you get back.

The voices in the head were giving him scratches in his head, -I don't know.

-C'mon Billy, don't take it like I don't love you anymore because I do. I just need time to figure out what I really want.

-Let's not talk about it. We'll settle it when I get back.

-O.k.

-*Go on my son.* Give Stacy me warmest regards.

-Do you want to come in?

-*To the kingdom, for Jesus will forgive all your sins.* Sure.

He took a seat near the girls, admiring the way their blonde hair and blue hands share the ocean and skies. They were even wearing similar clothes; clothes that they got for free thanks to Billy. They were two plus one, three separate parts. She began trying to whisper below the crowd noise, and Billy began to try to hear everything, all the while the sounds and voices became bitter sounds in his ears. He was still in the primary shock of the traumatic experience of losing his girl.

-*No. no nonononononono. Ughh. Yeah. We belong together; we are not separate parts. We belong together. I can't believe really wants to do this. I know she wants to break up. It's so she can fuck other guys. Don't think I'm stupid. I know how you think, you little piggy. Go on fuck those other guys while I'm away; see how far they take you. See if you are still as popular when you're eaten by a gator. Nobody in the industry will even acknowledge you, little piggy.*

Stacy and Casey turned their back to Billy. This pissed him off even more. Stacy wanted to know all the juicy details, -Hey, Casey, how did it go?

-*A holy ghost fantasizes about serenity. An allusion of philosophy not well taken. Sent to the lions by a gator.*

-He seemed to handle it great. A lot better than I expected. He didn't even freak out or anything.

Billy sat stewing quietly with a large beer in his hand. He began to feel alive; he had it on this side and the other side. Liquor felt better than sticking it in his veins. God felt bequeathed to the high; god felt better than the other side. -*It's over now. I'm all alone.*

Stacy felt a little relieved. She had the hots for Billy for a long time, and this was the perfect situation for her. She wanted him more than ever, now that her best friend did not have it anymore. Her addiction to sex stuck it into her veins, poisoned by Billy, -That's great, isn't it.

-*Possible my son that you should think about the consequences. I'm already dead. I've already created everything for the good, but now she's dead, too.*

-I guess so, Stacy, but do you think you can talk to him when he gets back from Vegas.

-*Maria will always be with you, even when you fell on the path of the beast. Remember, Jesus loves you.*

-What am I supposed to say to him?

Stacy knew what to say him. She will say anything to put him into bed, not unlike running water will do anything to get around every obstacle in its way; Stacy will do anything to get Billy.

-When I see him?

-When I see him, yeah. Just tell him that I want to still be friends.

-*I'm not going to be no friends. Sinner! That's what she is; she is a sinner. She probably never came down when we did; she'll come when I pray. I bet she will. Yes. That's what I want.*

-Do you think that's what Billy wants?

-What do you mean?

-Do you think he still wants to be your friend? Three years is a long time.

-*to hold something within you. Don't be afraid; I'm here to help.*

-He took it so well, though.

-I'll call him.

-Isn't Jesus always there?

-Please do.

-*Pray. You know he's there.*

-Do you want something to drink?

-Red wine.

-Give it time, Casey. Everything will work itself out.

-*Just tell me what happened.*

Well, during the rain last weekend, Casey and I went to Knott's because it best to go when it rains. Also, they do this thing called an "illegal hitchin'" performed by a Reverend Bean. We drove to Knott's through the storm to have some kicks. We both started on the mash, but when we arrived at Knott's, it was closed. We were kind of bummed; the novelty of the amusement park and the pseudo-marriage got us there. We thought the idea worked for that day. We looked at each other and realized that it didn't matter what were doing as long as we were doing it together. That was the craziest feeling I ever had in my stomach. We parked the car and decided to have a piece of pie and coffee. While we were eating the pie, Casey came up with a crazy idea, -Let's drive to Vegas and get married since we were supposed to do it today, anyway.

I forced down the pie, which was sitting dryly on my mouth, and gave a chuckle and replied, -All right. The moment was perfect. The weather was perfect for a long drive; the emotions were just right. And with my answer, Casey and I were on our way to Vegas to be married. We decide to not stop at home and get clothes because we felt it would ruin the spontaneity. We drove on the highway at 80 miles per hour in the rain. We figured to make an adventure out of it. We stopped at the nearest liquor store and bought some goods for the trip. Since Casey was driving she had a two liter bottle of coke; I had a one liter bottle of ginger ale and a pint of Jack's bourbon. For the actual wedding celebration, we bought a bottle of port wine. We raced to Vegas and were there in about four hours. The sky was so gray; rain got lost in the one-colored sky. We parked the car in the first parking lot we saw and began to walk around to find the best chapel. We passed a drive-thru chapels and such, but what really turned us on was a chapel where Elvis was the chaplain. We walked in the chapel. There were pink walls and a sign as we entered: Welcome to Graceland. We were greeted by a lady named Pricilla.

Stacy interrupted with irritation, -Dude. That is the worst fuckin' story I have ever heard. An Elvis chapel with Pricilla as the receptionist. Next, you're going to tell me that Lisa was the flower the girl.

Happily, surprised Billy continued, -Yeah. And the dog was named Marie. Anyway, it goes further. We walked to the sign-in book, and we signed our names. We waited for Elvis to do our wedding and listened to "Love Me Tender" over the intercom. After about forty-five minutes, it was our turn to get married.

Elvis called us up. He was classic. It was the old Elvis. He was about six feet three and weighed about 300 pounds. His breath smelled of alcohol, and he was slightly sweating on the brow and upper lip. His deep voice smoothed, "Billy Tod, do you lawfully take Casey Wilkes to be your wife?"

I replied, "I do."

Then he turned to Casey, "Now little lady, do you take this fine young gentleman to be your lawfully wedded husband?" Casey replied, "I do."

We were married in the eyes of God and Elvis. We drove home as quickly as possible. So, what do you think? I looked at the old lady pushing her shopping cart down the street. She maneuvered the cart perfectly. She drove it like an indy driver carefully manipulates the car to hug turns and pass everything in the way as if it were standing still.

Stacy frowned at me, so I had to ask, -Hey man, what do you think about my wedding?

Stacy smiled to cover her ire, but the smile lasted as quickly as the question. -What about it?

-What do you think about me getting married?

-Congratulations. I guess.

-But. I just got married.

-Why?

-It was something to do. It was for kicks.

-Are you in love with her?

-What are you gonna do when you get back?

-I guess I better be going.

There was only one message on Billy's machine when he got back,

-Gianni? This is Stacy. I want to talk to you about Casey. Umm, why don't you call me when you get back.

Billy sat looking out his window, not really thinking about anything. He just saw Santa Ana moving like underwater currents, a slow constant movement back and forth, methodical, smooth, with the grace of selfish love. *Love. Who am I to believe in this crazy concept of togetherness?*

Billy picked up the phone and quickly dialed Stacy's number, -Hello? Is Stacy home?

She responded, -Speaking. Billy? I've been waiting for you to call.

-Hi . . . Stacy. . . . This is Billy.

-Hey Billy . . . listen, I wanted to talk with you about Casey, and how she feels about you. She wanted me to talk to you when you got back.

-Why can't she talk to me herself? *No one is ever there to listen. I just wanted some answers.*

-Well, she is kind of busy lately, but she does want you call her now that you're home. Anyway, when can you get together so we can talk.

-*Without hesitation. God is always listening. Even when we can't see the sky's scenery.* Why don't we go out to dinner Saturday night?

-Perfect.

-All right. I'll see you then.

-O.k. see you later, Billy.

-*Are you sure you want to go on? You do have an option to leave and come back when you are fully ready to accept Jesus in your life. Then everything will be o.k.* O.k. See ya, Casey.

Stacy stated with benevolence, -Stacy.

-Yeah . . . Stacy.

I picked her up in the white convertible Caddy.

-Where are we going?

-I thought we could eat at The Shrimp Steamer.

-Aren't you a vegetarian?

-Not anymore, baby.

At The Shrimp Steamer, *Carrie*Stacy ate her crab linguine with such etiquette. She was almost prissy about getting herself dirty. Billy just stuck the crab legs between the tongs and crushed them. Hard. Sometimes he squeezed them so hard the meat wasn't edible because it had shells all over them. He ate it anyway; he just crunched away; it was pretty good, too. The mashing of the shells between the teeth made him feel like he could break rocks. They didn't talk much over dinner. To get all of his crazy anxiety out of his system, Billy suggested they take a drive along the coast.

-Sure. But promise you'll want to talk about Stacy.

-Sure thing, baby.

The two drove down the coast toward Laguna. The top was down, the cool summer beach air whispered in their hair. The music felt like warm showers beading through their heads. After about thirty minutes, Billy pulled into the Sugar Shack. It was a cool spot to watch the boats pass in the summer nights. They could be alone and talk about the differences with Billy and Carrie. But first, Billy wanted a kiss.

-No, Billy.

-C'mon. just give me one kiss baby.

-No. Get off me.

-You're going to kiss me baby.

Then Billy gave her a small quick *peck*punch *on*in the nose. She didn't even start to bleed that much.

-You Fucker.

-You're going to kiss me and like it.

He started *kissing*hitting her even harder. It felt good to let loose. The more she resisted, the more he felt like laying it into her.

-What gives you the right to break up with me? You just want to go out and fuck other guys, huh? Do you think you can fool me, you little piggy?

After about two minutes of *kissing*punching her in the face, she stopped resisting. Stacy just leaned back in the chair. Billy thought she tried fooling him by playing dead, but he also thought he knew better. He saw the blood bubble with every breath. He sat back for a moment and lit a smoke; he needed the rest. All the hitting made him sort of tired. All he could think about was that fucking song by The Smiths (Marr & Morrissey, 1986):

> oh ho sweetness
> I was only joking
> when I said
> I'd like to mash
> every tooth in your head.

The lyrics kept echoing and echoing; they were a skipping lp paralyzed by the suspended movements of weakness.

Billy quickly took Stacy's top off of her and lifted her skirt to pull down her thong. He put out his smoke on a small puddle near her ear. He put his dick inside her dry vagina; she felt the rod of death being laid in her; it was her last feeling. It was a last feeling of complete helplessness; a feeling of complete sympathy overcame her as she walked into the area of the world's memories to find hers.

Billy loved it; he thought he was the man. He was the person she loved; she couldn't leave; she will always be back. She had no right to break up with him. *She was being selfish, and I know she isn't like that. She loves every moment we have together, just as she loves every moment we are experiencing together right now.* Billy turned her over on her face and spread her arms and legs to make it look like she passed out drunk face down. *You've always liked it like this. You want it harder don't you. Let me make it easier on the both of us.*

Billy walked around to the passenger side of the car and took a quick look at himself in the glare of the waxed paint. He took a long look at his reflection, and he felt beautiful. He could see the black ocean and the black sky behind him. He opened the door and cautiously stepped into the car. *You love it, don't you? You love it, huh? YOU LOVE IT, DONTCHA?* He felt her smooth blonde hair and caressed it a little. It was pretty and soft despite the wetness. And he kneeled there looking at the maroon-glazed, blonde hair glistening in the full moon light. *How could we do this with as little blood as possible? I think it is better this way. That way you don't get pregnant and breed without me.*

He grabbed her hair head and put it in the door jam. He tried to close the door three times. Softly at first, but it just needed to be harder. It was not hard enough to actually crush it the first time, but hard enough to hurt what little she had left. Each time, he slammed the door a little harder. *That's it baby. That ought to do it. That's it; right there.*

Billy finished the job with minimal blood on his clothes. A little blood on the shoes, but shoes to Billy were a dime a dozen. He got three free pair every month. Alone, Billy snapped out of it. He felt listless at his own violence. All he could think was what to do with the body.

At the time, there was construction going on across P.C.H. Back behind the first hill, there was a small skateboard ditch that could be ridden. It wasn't that good, but it did throw out some good grinds; plus, any hikers would never go up that way. He drove her up there, and using his skateboard like a shovel, buried her about three feet down.

He drove back down the hill and slowly drove home.

There was a message on Billy's answering machine when he got back home.

-Hey, Billy. This is Randall. There's a gig at Club Decca tonight. Duane's band is playing with the Tramps. Give me call when you get home.

The phone rang during the message.

- Billy?

-Casey?

-No. This is Stacy.

-Oh shit.

-I wanted to see how your talk with Casey went.

-Umm. I didn't go out with her.

-Why?

-Son, are you sure want to continue? Is this all the truth.

-I don't know. I've been trying to call her all night. Actually, I thought you were her. Have you spoken with her tonight?

-No. I just called her and she's not home.

-Well, since she is nowhere to be found, do you want to go to Club Decca tonight and see Duane's band?

-Well, I was going out with Stacy when she got home with you, but I guess I can leave a message for her to meet us there.

-I can't let you know the information because I can't think about it, but it is itching my brain. I must confess. But first, I must ask you if God forgives?

Billy washed his hands and threw away his clothes. He decided to take the motorcycle due to the minor blood stains on the vinyl and door jam.

-Clean up when I get home. *Now.* Yeah, clean up now. Good ole Casey can wait five minutes.

The blood wiped right off with a little 409, and the door jamb wasn't as bad as he originally thought. He put a tree on the rear-view mirror and hopped on the motorcycle to get Stacey*Casey.*

Chapter Five

Poetry as Reflections

Whereas there is an exactness and purposefulness to art, poetry is an art that asks the artist to be exact in diction and style. In this book, poetry gives the reader wonderful, fluid diction that breaks the separation of fact and fiction. Using poetry as a powerful method for reflection as data is not a new avenue (Leavy, 2015; Subramanian in Cahnmann-Taylor & Siegesmund, 2018). Poems give a unique sense of freedom and constriction; poetry allows the human experience to be revealed by using sensory details, so the writer becomes a painter using words as their color palate and the keyboard as the canvas. As a result, poetry gives the reader a unique method to reveal data through the power of words and voice.

Poetry representation is recognized qualitative source that allows all of the participants an alternative to traditional sources of data. Even though data may be unverifiable and seem disadvantageous, one's life and experiences need multiple sources of data, including poetry, for poetry gives insight to the human experience, insight that science can't ever express (Shapiro, 2004). Thus, the writer and reader can take a poem and interpret different meanings and give a more closely relevant interpretation to how the poem shows the actual human experience and the influence of the experience on one's life.

This text includes poems to become a representation of the voice making a commentary on social consciousness. Using poetry allows one to capture and reveal the true humanness that exists within the incarcerated and formerly incarcerated population (Percer, 2002). The poems bring in the tenets of their lives and social criticisms that fuse an anger and humanness. Similarly, to narrative inquiry, poems can be deconstructed using Arts Based Research with elements of literary analysis to show the ethnographic underlining of the purposeful social commentary. Poetry representation as recognized qualitative revelations give the reader an additional benefit than simply reading for pleasure. This merging of craft adds to Arts Based Research. More so, poetry gives theoretical insights that fall under the postmodern and post structural theoretical perspectives.

The ability to show how poems reflect the human experience is important in this book because the purpose of this book *is* to address the human experience. This merging of poetry and the human experience add to Arts Based Research. So, using poetry as a reflection of the human experience allows poetry to be "a vehicle through which to communicate powerful and multiple 'truths' about the human experience" (Furman, Langer, Davis, Gallardo, & Kulkarni, 2007, p. 302). With the emergence of looking at poetry in this light, alternative theoretical developments emerged as well, giving all participants a fresh perspective on how to look at the poems as more than words as data; thus, breaking the dynamics of the traditional approach to study and introducing academia to poetic inquiry. Spending time musing over poems gives a significant meaning to the poem; it allows the poet to feel and give their emotions using a lyrical paintbrush. Lahman, Geist, Rodriguez, Graglia, Richard, & Schendel (2010, p. 44) indicate a similar sentiment: "It seems the effect of time spent discussing poetry over six months had a deepening impact on the meaning each person conveyed and was evidenced in the tone and tenor of the . . . contributions."

Galvan and Prendergast (2016) further the legitimacy of poetry as inquiry by expressing that poetry allows for finding lush, comprehensive avenues to relay findings. Prendergast (2009) shows poetic inquiry expresses three main data as reflective of the human experience, all centered around voice:

1. Vox Autobiographia/Autoethnographia (Researcher-voice): researchers produce the data from observations, interviews, and ethnographic research. It includes all forms of poetry and is primarily an autobiographical type of poetry framed in the context of the researcher. Then, the researcher presents their data.
2. Vox Participare (Participant-voice): this process allows the researcher to take the participant's "voice" into account when producing the work. The participant writes the poem entirely, or the poem is co-constructed with the researcher.
3. Vox Theoria (Literature-voice): similar to "found poetry," this method uses literature and/or theory as the primary source of creation of poetry. Literature-voiced poetry speaks to the understanding of the audience and research.

Of the three, this book focuses primarily on "Vox Autobiographia/ Autoethnographia (Researcher-voice)" method. After numerous interviews and observations, including member checking, constructing poems seems the most transparent form of reflecting voice. Also, I felt that me being able to identify with the students' lives because I lived a very similar life to theirs allowed me to attempt to write their experiences as a poem.

At the very root of poetry, it is emotion. Social reflections through poetry have an unconscious foundation in emotion. Since social reflections has emotion as a foundation, social reflections need a deeper relationship (Carbado & Roithmayr, 2014) with its participants, a deeper relationship that only poetry can provide. Using deductive reasoning, poetry can be used to evoke the emotion and critical theories of social research concurrently. Yet poetry has a unique way of making the data more accessible to the public; in other words, scientific knowledge can be relayed to the public through poetry (Leavy, 2015). It "reveals a moment of truth" (Leavy, 2015, p. 77). It gives the opportunity to use data for identity and the human experience by revealing "multiple meanings" (Leavy, 2015).

Further, poetry allows one to make the connection between identity and marginalized populations. As a result, poetry will be used in this book to make the connection between the human/educational experience in education; and an artistic reflection of the relationship between the human/educational experience, identity, and society. The poems in this text bring in the emotive tenets that fuse an anger and humanness with the reality of the incarcerated juvenile's situation and experience. Similar to narrative inquiry, poems can be deconstructed using Arts Based Research with elements of literary analysis to show the ethnographic underlining of the purposeful social commentary.

Poetry is emotion. Poetry, then, has an unconscious foundation in emotion; moreover, the juvenile justice experience—personal and educational—and their relationships evoke emotion. Yet poetry has a unique way of making the data more accessible to the public; in other words, scientific knowledge can be relayed to the public through poetry (Leavy, 2015). It "reveals a moment of truth" (Leavy, 2015, p. 77). It gives the opportunity to use poems for identity by revealing "multiple meanings" (Leavy, 2015). Further, poetry allows the author and reader to make the connection between identity and marginalized populations. The potential for poetry to be used in academia is limitless, and the reader has the ability to use this art as a method for representing data. The following three poems give a sense of emotion and experience that furthers the data presented at the beginning of this text.

POETIC INQUIRY ANALYSIS OF
ARTISTIC REFLECTIONS

The poems address Leavy's claims several times during the poem. First, the poems address the "moment of truth" throughout the poems, beginning with the titles: "Screaming Down the 5 With Steve," "Born Free," and "A Freedom Unrealized." The titles indicate that the epiphanic experiences about the meaning of freedom, and the importance freedom holds in one's life. In

"Screaming Down the 5 With Steve," the protagonist indicates that he and his friend experience literal freedom by having the ability to speed on the freeway; also, there is an emotional freedom that is shared with his friend. "Born Free" indicates a freedom by right, but the protagonist chooses to juxtapose an irony by having the poet explicate on how he and those like him are not "free." In "A Freedom Unrealized," the title gives the reader the ability to identify with one's freedom by examining how one cannot understand the privilege of freedom until freedom is jeopardized.

Additionally, and similarly to the fictive narratives, the "moment of truth" significance is present in all three poems:

"Screaming Down the 5 With Steve"

- she treated me like an adult in a world of/children
- talking about our neighborhood/all the bright things/and the brightness

"Born Free"

- from the beginning your presence was devasting
- so I won't celebrate america's arrival
- wasted. you perpetuate the lie of the American society;/I am not free

"A Freedom Unrealized"

- I walked/through doors/and doors/to get/to a classroom/whose roof/was covered/in barbed wire;
- I realized/I don't need/to ask/for permission/to go outside/and feel/the sun/on my skin;
- I realized/one mistake/could take it/a w a y

The poems, collectively, address two meanings: freedom and truth. The idea of freedom is ambiguous until freedom is taken away, or the idea of freedom is questioned. It is at the point of losing freedom that the protagonists realize that freedom is not an abstract idea, but it is a real feeling and a real concept. The idea of confinement plays a significant role throughout the poem. The protagonists understand that the contrast between confinement and freedom are directly opposed to each other. The realization of confinement, or incarceration, holds several realities that are used to make the author realize that incarceration can hold traumatic events within it. For example, the protagonist's reference to asking for permission to use the bathroom illustrates the concept of incarceration. Another example is the visualization of the classroom's perimeter surrounded by barbed wire; this presents a dark, mentally suffocating view of learning. The poems successfully attempt to draw a connection between the readers and the incarcerated populations, and the use of realistic details creates and supports the identity and voice of juvenile justice education life.

POEMS

The first poem reflects on friendship and relationships. The initial draft of the poem was two poems. One was about a car ride with "Steve"; the other was about a relationship with his girlfriend. During our interviews, the incarcerated student indicated that he was about to "lose" his girlfriend because of the amount of time he did. He had a real anxiety about maintaining the relationship. After reading the poems, I revised the original two poems and merged them to create one exposition of protagonist's thoughts about "Steve" and his "love." After the second draft, I introduced the incarcerated student to e.e. cummings, and I asked him what he thought of the author, and there was a respect for the succinctness of cummings. I revised the poem to a third draft to follow the style of cummings. The incarceratd student and I felt this was the best draft.

This second poem was written as a response to Langston Hughes's "Let America Be America Again." This poem exudes the anger and anxiety as a reaction to one of the great poems of last century. The idea for this poem came after having a conversation about how the formerly incarcerated student was having a difficult time finding a job due to his incarceration. And the jobs that he did find were all part-time employment, so he had to get two part-time jobs and was in the process of looking for a third. This left little to no time for school, academic or vocational. The catch-22 situation led to this poem. The first draft of the poem had no capitalization, with the intent to not capitalize "america" to show protest. I thought that I should keep the lack of capitalization, yet I should capitalize "I" to indicate his feelings of isolation and abandonment by his country. The second draft was centered for stylistic purposes.

The last poem was inspired by an intern in the program, Sarah. Sarah had never heard of Arts Based Research, and I explained the philosophy behind Arts Based Research and my intentions with the poem and why poems are an important methodology for reflections. The development of the poem took on a two-part process. The first draft was a traditional poem, left justified on the page. I thought the reflection of the facility gave a unique insight to the different experience with both education and life with the two individuals. Upon further exploration, I found that Sarah was deeply "justice impacted" and that the use of poetry allowed for me to help her identify with how her life was affected by friends and family who were incarcerated. For this poem, I used "Vox Participare"; Sarah submitted a poem, and my suggestions were to center it and write the last word to look like it fades to the right margin. For my part, I made the poem more concise by closely editing and centering only precise words.

POEMS AS REFLECTIONS

"Screaming Down the 5 with Steve"

blind lights of cars stream by at 120 mph
steve and I rolled in the black Jetta
talking about the workplace

everybody in it
we came to one agreement;

one girl shines above all the rest
I really dug her compassion when the clouds
were gray and the streets were black
we kissed for one night
it was a two-year one-night stand

it was good
she treated me like an adult in a world of
children

steve liked her smile
and the way she jokes around with him;
he says she makes him laugh
he says she has humor, which is good

in a place full of actors playing the role,

most of them will remain actors to me and steve
I like the original smile too
I guess that is why we hang out, me and steve,
we kind of dig on the same things
the light shines off the hurricane as I break a promise
and I laugh because she thinks I am trouble
I like to play, yeah
but I like for people to take me seriously, too
compassion, yeah. humor, yeah

and steve and I drive 120 mph down the 5
talking about our neighborhood
and everything in it
and everybody in it
all the bright things

and the brightness in it
I need to close my eyes for this love
I swear to god
so I laugh again as she walks by in my thoughts
tee hee

"Born Free"

it's a disease made like heroin's hype

we are in the mind set to celebrate this disease.
from the beginning your presence was devastating.
so I won't celebrate america's arrival;
I won't celebrate the AIDS or the flu;

because it is all a celebration of you.
wasted.
you perpetuate the lie of the american society;
I am not free in this democracy.
I became possessed

in the new world to work in a slave society.
I am taught today
and day by day to respect the environment,
but it is the earth which deserves me respect.
to come into harmony with the universe,
the environment was tortured, now feared.
we are ready to understand
the ancient thought of my ancestors:

"be at peace with the earth."
I lost my spiritual identity
with religious identification;
beads of christ ran down my forehead,
but was never under my skin.

I was born free.
I see no humanity
in a country that treats me the way she does;
I tried to breathe in the uncomfortable land;
to see, and to survive in this god-loving country,

in this murderous god-loving country.

death came to my people along with christianity.

no humanity. as for the holidays—
meaningless.
I have no natural rights, no freedom.
what is there to celebrate
I can't celebrate where I'm from,
to celebrate the discovery of a new drug,
a new addictive high as potent as heroin and crack,
to celebrate this flu
is to be connected with this old addictive chain.
I will not smoke the disease,
nor will I let it travel through my veins.
taught to say "no,"
I say, "no," to a celebration
of disease and unnatural drugs

created when my spirit was lost.
my spirit will not survive
in this hardened witchcraft and wise men,
nor does it want to.
I came into myself
to stop spreading the disease

"A Freedom Unrealized"

I
never really gave
much thought
about what freedom is

and what it means to me
Until
I walked
through doors
and doors
to get
to a classroom
whose roof
was covered

in barbed wire
I never
really gave
much thought
about what freedom
is
and what

it means to me
Until
I realized
I don't need
to ask
for permission
to go outside
and feel

the sun
on my skin
I never
really gave
much thought about
what freedom is
and what
it means to me
Until
I realized
one mistake
could take it
a
     w
       a
         y

Chapter Six

Rehabilitate the Rehabilitation

Recently, legislative and academic communities have moved forward with efforts to improve rehabilitative efforts for incarcerated individuals. Agencies can implement a stronger prosperous community by offering more alternatives for incarcerated juveniles (Sanders, 2021). While there is sufficient research for adult education and educational services for incarcerated individuals, there is limited literature on postsecondary academic opportunities for incarcerated juveniles that goes beyond quantitative methods of inquiry; in other words, the research is driven by number-laden data. Qualitative data is necessary to know and understand the human value of the people caught up in juvenile justice. Research needs to address the issues that need focus: the lives and voices that lead juveniles to incarceration and correcting the variables that lead to crime and punishment.

Further, less literature exists on the academic experience of incarcerated juveniles; rather, the literature focuses on the causes of negative experiences that lead to the school to prison pipeline, not on qualitative ethnographic narratives that could reveal insights for establishing more productive, positive academic environments. The work that this book concentrated on an uniquely analyzing a small set of such experiences by giving voice to a population that has consistently had their voice silenced before, during, and after incarceration as well as within their K–12 academic experience. Recognizing and giving light to voices that have traditionally been silenced revolutionizes the essence of critical pedagogy. Education needs to become the voice of the incarcerated juvenile.

The purpose of writing this text was to explore how participating in a university driven postsecondary program affected long-term incarcerated juveniles' perceptions of academia. But the narratives revealed that the factors influencing perceptions of academia go far beyond the school grounds. The incarcerated and formerly incarcerated students in this text revealed that school falls in priority; school is just one factor in the school to prison pipeline. On the one hand, the findings helped to answer some principal questions about working with incarcerated juveniles. Questions that addressed the perceptions incarcerated juveniles had about academia after participating in a higher education program that drew from culturally relevant pedagogy and students' funds of knowledge were answered through qualitative research, but those answers did not address the real issue that surfaced. The conversations and reflections showed that outside factors influenced the students much more in-depth than a desire for academic advancement.

Once the factors were expressed through the narrative reflections, the students became more receptive to "voicing" in class, and their perceptions of academia changed positively. As a result, the students' prior held perceptions were significantly changed—mindset if you will—about learning and understanding of academia, their sense of voice, their relations with college aged peers, and how life choices matter. Thus, the input of the juvenile hall academic administrator who runs the secondary academic program was recruited as well in order to complete the picture of the perceptions of the students and academia; on a secondary level, the administrator's story illustrated the sort of support network that is available within a juvenile correctional facility.

The use of fictive narratives and poems was chosen not only to honor the voices of participants but to provide a nontraditional attempt at relaying their experiences. Fictive narratives and poems invite the reader to have a better understanding of the academic experiences of the participants by allowing the reader, the researcher, and the participant to unconsciously reflect on elements of their lives and experiences. The narratives in this text bring forward the voices of the various participants; it juxtaposes their experience with artwork through a creative perspective.

Though there exists literature addressing the secondary academic experience of the incarcerated juvenile, the relevant literature about postsecondary education for incarcerated juveniles is limited, primarily since the postsecondary options for incarcerated is limited. Reviewing the literature that addressed the secondary academic experience for the incarcerated juvenile shows limited opportunities for the incarcerated juvenile; also, it shows that there is a gap in the literature between secondary education and adult education for incarcerated individuals. The literature provides a foundation for the school to prison pipeline, a pathway lower socioeconomic people of color are far too familiar with. The literature also addresses the attempts to disrupt the school to prison pipeline, but current literature does not touch on the influence of higher education on reducing recidivism for incarcerated juveniles.

A limited amount of literature addressing and showing the efficacy of higher education with incarcerated juveniles can only begin the conversation of effective academic pedagogy for incarcerated juveniles by first attempting to address the failures in the incarcerated students' previous academic understanding and juxtaposing it with an alternative, a more rigorous and culturally relevant academic experience. Additionally, it must reflect on their personal, life experiences to get an understanding of how to bring a more effective educational experience, for example, Culturally Responsive Teaching and Funds of Knowledge. Using the Culturally Responsive Teaching and Funds of Knowledge approach provides a positive model for higher education that apparently has been missing in the incarcerated students' experience. Bottom line: we need to know the human stories, not just the numbers.

Thus, the ideology needs to be centered on strengthening society through accessible higher education for incarcerated adults and allowing participants to experience an equitable academic environment. Providing an equitable academic environment led to four major conclusions: recognizing the experience of the individual, recognizing the impact of the experience, recognizing the development of relationships, and recognizing the voice of the individuals.

THE GREAT DIVIDER? OR EQUALIZER?: THE EDUCATIONAL EXPERIENCE

Knowing the stories helps with changing the perceptions of higher education because knowing the stories change the pedagogy. The educational experience was a major factor with the individuals because it allowed the students to begin to understand that their voice was important. Being able to voice one's opinions and thoughts in a safe, welcoming classroom allowed for the individuals to be more receptive to establishing their voice creatively and vice versa. While establishing the voice was primarily driven by the students, the inclusion of the academic administrator in this analysis allowed for him to also give his perspective because academic administrators play a role in supporting and observing the educational experience throughout academia. The formerly incarcerated students' perspectives emerged through the interviews and artistic representations.

The emerging voice vis-à-vis the educational experience finding suggests that educational experiences prior to participating in the higher education program left little to be desired, from the initiation of their comprehensive schooling to correctional education. The written reflections revealed the participants' negative perspectives on their prior life experience that led to their negative mindset about education. Interestingly, the written reflections led to a transformation as well. Analyzing the fictive narratives and poetry enhanced the stories and poems by also pointing to the importance of reflection on previous experiences and using that to change the pedagogy that could more effectively be used with incarcerated youth.

This led to the intrinsic value of a Culturally Responsive Teaching and Funds of Knowledge pedagogical approach. Images and words from the artistic submissions gave the perception that up until the higher education experience, the incarcerated students had dominantly negative experiences in life and education. The teacher can use the words and experiences of the students as a pedagogical diving board to honor the experiences and use the experiences to incorporate and develop a curricular pathway for the students. Consequently, the students receive a more personalized curriculum that addresses and respects the students' experiences, while providing relevant curriculum that adheres to school and state guidelines for learning.

THE DIVIDED PATH IN THE CONCRETE
FOREST: LIFE AND ITS IMPACT

"Life" and its impact emerged and reflected how for most of the participants, life presented situations where they made a choice about which direction to take, and subsequently, affected their academic trajectory. The theme revealed the foundation for the divergent choices and pathway about academia with the formerly incarcerated youth. In other words, their life experience led them to have a moment where they gave up; I like the call it the "Fuck It" moment.

In context, life and its impact started to emerge with the students who were already in the path of the school to prison pipeline, though an interesting observation surfaced as I went through the process of writing and revision. While going through the fictive narrative and poetry analysis, there was a connection between the incarcerated and formerly incarcerated students' life and the academic experience alignment with the school to prison pipeline, and somehow their decisions in their life reflected in the academic experience. Interestingly, the formerly incarcerated students were on the margins of the school to prison pipeline because they each had an experience with the school to prison pipeline. For example, almost every person referenced in this text saw their friends and relatives get caught in the school to prison pipeline, so being involved in the criminal justice system became the norm rather than the outlier. The importance of education may have been reinforced by the family, but the prevalence of the criminal justice experience within their lives outweighed any educational priority, thereby reinforcing the benefits of a life of criminality over a path toward academia. Unfortunately, in nearly everyone's experience, including mine, they saw how the school to prison pipeline could also lead to a fatal ending, either by a literal death or a lifetime incarcerated.

Contrary to the "Fuck It" moment, within most experiences, whether that of the inmate or academic, there was a significant moment when each participant made a conscious decision about being focused on academia. Because of negative academic and life experiences, the student inmates decided that ultimately resulted in their incarceration. Similarly, each of the formerly incarcerated juveniles experienced an intervention that changed their academic experience to a more positive one. It was the difference in these two types of experiences that resulted in a major, life-defining moment. Upon their reflection, the higher education program also became the much-needed intervention for the student inmates. In summary, the life experiences of the student inmates influenced their choices toward education and how that feeling translated into their lives outside of academia. Similarly, the experiences of the students in the higher education program showed how their academic experiences translated into their lives inside and outside of academia. Each participant discovered that participating in the higher education program changed their perceptions overall. The formerly incarcerated students' perceptions of academia changed because they experienced a more progressive form of education versus the essentialist education commonly practiced in juvenile justice and urban education. The formerly incarcerated students' perception of academia was widened, for they participated in an educational experience beyond one they had ever experienced within the walls of their life and incarceration.

FINDING THE GLUE

One of the more interesting themes that emerged was that of relationships; relationships mattered, even if it was a relationship was just one-to-one. This theme was critical to the students' transformational experience. The transformational experience in the perception of academia began as the formerly incarcerated student inmates, teachers, and staff developed friendships. When the participating groups became familiar with each other on a psychological connection, this bond played what seemed a significant role in the impact of the higher education program, for example, the ending of "Viejito" where Old Man Dios remembers Bridget. The groups created a bond within an alternative educational structure. Essentially, employing and recognizing voice concurrently with a Culturally Responsive Teaching and Funds of Knowledge pedagogy made the insider-outsider relationship more transparent. Interestingly, the incarcerated student inmates began to feel like outsiders within the incarceration facility because they were considered "college students" while still maintaining insider status in the facility walls.

Participating in a somewhat "normal" academic program created a sense of normalcy for the students while they were considered inmates; it made them feel as if for that brief period of the day while in the course, they were not incarcerated. This feeling helped in providing a more "normalized" academic experience. One student lamented during an interview: "I loved going to the classes. I felt like I was actually learning. I felt like I was actually in school. It was the only time during the entire week where I felt normal. I was able to take that feeling back to the cell with me and feel normal while I was doing work. It felt good." For some, this was the first time they had experienced what many of us would consider what is expected from an academic experience.

After release, the student inmates continued their peer-to-peer relationships with each other. The fact that the relationships continued after the student inmates were released shows the significance of the connection. Most of the formerly incarcerated participants continued to pursue higher education and were no longer as intimidated by the complex structure of college. The members and participants of the higher education program helped to forge the friendships. While this data is incalculable through quantitative means, the artistic reflections showed qualitatively how the development and perception of relationships is important in the lives of at-promise students and could influence their educational experience.

FROM LOUD WHISPER TO SILENT ROAR

Finding one's voice is difficult, especially when that voice is consistently suppressed. It seems that the suppression of voice happens frequently in traditional education; and as a result, the students who experience the school to prison pipeline tend to silence their voices even more and in different ways. A pivotal moment in the process of writing this book was when the students began to express their own voices. It is one thing to have independent, critical thought, but it is something entirely different to express those thoughts without fear or anxiety. Student inmates were quiet at the beginning of the program, but two important events occurred that gave them a greater sense of voice. The first was participating in a higher education program that honored their voices and experiences. The emergence of voice and its influence on the academic experience brought their experience to the "inside" walls of the correctional facility and encouraged the (then) incarcerated student to express their voices from the inside as well.

The second was when the incarcerated student noticed they could express their thoughts without repercussions. This recognition gave them the courage to begin expressing their voices and asking critical inquiry questions authentically without fear of disciplinary action. This sentiment was supported by one of the student inmates beginning to ask critical questions to people of authority. Here is a brief account of the exchange that became the defining moment of the emerging voice:

During one of the guest lecture presentations, the guest lecturer concluded by stating, "Thank you for having me. This has been a pleasant surprise."

Although the lecturer did not mean any ill-will with this statement, one of incarcerated students raised his hand, "Can I ask you a question? What did you mean by that?"

The lecturer was taken aback. She really did not know how to answer the question. In fact, the whole class was quiet. The other incarcerated students did not know what to make of the question. They were waiting for the Deputy Probation Officer (DPO) to correct and reprimand the student (NOTE: the DPO was in the class every week and was familiar and supportive of what we were doing in the class and the class dynamics). They all looked at the DPO like "What are you going to do?" The DPO just shrugged his shoulders and smiled. The incarcerated student continued, "You are the third guest we have had, and you all have said the same thing. 'You were pleasantly surprised.' What did you expect when you came in here?"

The guest lecturer understood what the incarcerated student was asking, and she answered openly and honestly. The conversation expanded to include what others expected when they entered an incarcerated facility and how television and movies skew the perception of incarcerated facilities. Other incarcerated students joined into the conversation; even the DPO joined the conversation. Overall, the student who respectfully spoke up *broke a barrier*. He understood that it was okay to question, and the other students comprehended the intentionality of the question and the conversation to be a form respectful conversation. From that class onward, the students became more involved in the classroom discussion; the class became less didactic and more constructive.

The emergence of voice became an expansion of thought. The incarcerated students felt a freedom that was otherwise stifled in their current situation, a freedom that was reflected in the artistic representations of the participants by being able to recognize their voice and taking the recognition into the academic environment.

WHAT NOW?

This book began because I felt that students who participated in the juvenile justice system had a voice that needed to be heard. The text and writings grew because my interest in expanding postsecondary options for long-term incarcerated juveniles grew as a result of hearing and learning their stories. The recognition of the lack of postsecondary academic opportunities for long term incarcerated juveniles led to questioning whether providing postsecondary academic opportunities could impact incarcerated juveniles' perceptions about academia. Two main conclusions could be drawn from the experience:

1. juveniles who are/were incarcerated experienced significant traumatic life experiences that affected their perceptions about life and school and
2. school became an outlet and source for them to find their academic voice.

Consequently, participating in a nontraditional postsecondary academic program positively affects the incarcerated and formerly incarcerated juveniles' mindset and perceptions about higher education. This is especially true given that the experience included positive inter-relationship building with the students, instructors, administrators, and staff that allowed the students to understand the importance for the emergence of student voice.

What we all learned was that there are several benefits for incarcerated juveniles in having a legitimate postsecondary academic program. Juvenile justice postsecondary education benefits the incarcerated student by providing multiple higher education curricular options. The possibility of a student attending college loses its small glimmer of hope once that student becomes incarcerated, especially when attempting to shed the stigma and memory of negative academic experience after negative academic experience. Once the students understood the availability of higher education and, more importantly, the possibility of attending a university, the motivation toward obtaining higher education became more focused on succeeding academically. Incarcerated students became more interested in their grades and feedback; they exhibited behaviors that are commonly attributed to the more privileged student. In addition, they stopped exhibiting behaviors that had originally led them to the school to prison pipeline. The students changed their views on higher education by having an educational experience more parallel to a typical meaning-centered university experience.

Other correlations that surfaced were the benefits to peer relationship building and its effects on the educational experience. When the incarcerated students were encouraged to develop academic relationships, they began to understand some of the benefits of the entire academic experience. They developed a special collegiality that was embraced by the incarcerated students those around them. Interestingly, the creation of "friendships" became the most motivating, most significant factor in the success of the incarcerated student once they became the formerly incarcerated student. All the incarcerated students in the higher education program seemed to learn more deeply as a consequence of creating these academic friendships that transcended beyond the prison walls.

The experiences of everyone in this text provide new insights into juvenile justice education because the text suggests that focusing on the "school" in the school to prison pipeline is narrow and limiting. The current literature suggested that one factor in juvenile justice education was the relationship between learning and behavior. This was supported when probation staff noted that students in the unit (housing cell units for the juveniles) changed their behavior as a result of participating in the higher education program. The officers noted that the students had a definite interest in attending the college program, and the students understood that the program was available to those with positive behavior in the unit. As a result, the students in the program displayed positive behaviors, were more involvement in beneficial extracurricular activities, and became a positive influence on the other juveniles in their unit.

These apparent beneficial consequences proved worthy for the incarcerated student because every student who had the ability to argue for his case to be tried in juvenile court was granted his petition and allowed for his release from incarceration. While this happened before the fictive narratives and poems were constructed, in my view, this was a major impact because most of the students were facing major time if they would have been convicted as an adult.

The implications for society to benefit from such efforts go beyond the reduction of criminal behavior by juveniles; the implication that students' lives influence their academics surfaces throughout the fictive narratives. The probability for recidivism greatly decreases in correlation to the amount of education one receives while he or she is incarcerated. In other words, the more education an incarcerated student experiences, the less likely they will commit crimes after release from incarceration. Former inmates with little to no education typically do not have financial resources to help them or educational training to get jobs; therefore, they have a propensity to commit more crimes (Bender, 2018). A second implication is financial. With higher education, the probability to earn more money over a lifetime increases. Smith (2019) indicates that the former inmates who enrolled in an educational program while incarcerated had an increase employment rate by 10 percent and increased their comprehensive wage earnings by $45.3 million in their first year of postincarceration. Social benefits resulting from the advance of postsecondary education for incarcerated juveniles can have major positive consequences to the individual and society.

Logic, then, dictates that higher education institutions need to affirm and advocate positively for the provision of a postsecondary education program for long-term incarcerated juveniles who have graduated high school. One overall implication is that a Culturally Relevant Teaching and a Funds of Knowledge pedagogy that centers on the student experiences has positive outcomes for incarcerated youth and their education. This includes, but is not limited to, the participation of peer student/mentors from universities that host the classes. In addition, the higher education model gives insights and understanding to how college for incarcerated juveniles might be designed in the future. It exposes an effective pedagogical approach for educating individuals who have had prior negative schooling experiences. A culturally relevant and critical education gives a sense of "normalcy" to students who have experienced an abnormal education for most of their lives. Finally, and most importantly, postsecondary education for incarcerated juveniles encourages and gives these students an avenue of hope in what is otherwise a dark world where the sense of hope is just a four-letter word.

This book set forth attempting to identify the efficacy of an alternative pedagogy with formerly long-term incarcerated juveniles and culturally relevant, critical postsecondary education for incarceration juveniles. However, prior to addressing some of the conclusions for higher education for incarcerated and formerly incarcerated juveniles, it is necessary point to several other areas that need attention. Future work with incarcerated and formerly incarcerated juveniles need to look at the school to prison pipeline more comprehensively, with a paradigm shift toward more positive interventions, relationship building, and increasing the availability of academic and social options.

The prism of the school to prison pipeline needs further study. Rather than continue to merely focus on the school to prison pipeline's negative effects on students and the role of the school to prison pipeline as the pathway to prison, we need to examine the nature of how educators and programs interface within the school to prison pipeline. If the various facets, effects, and triggers of the pipeline are better understood, then academia needs to focus on changing the pedagogical paradigm, identifying, and concentrating on how academia can possibly help to address student needs before they land in juvenile hall or even after the fact. The efficacy of the higher education program in juvenile hall was founded on changing the academic experience of incarcerated juveniles because

1. it is a travesty that academic institutions continue to address students who learn differently similarly to how they address students 100 years ago,
2. it is inexcusable to continue to assume that students assimilate similarly to the expectations of 50 years ago, and
3. it is detrimental to administer punishment similarly to how it was done historically, knowing the efficacy of crime and punishment.

Academia also needs to change how it addresses students from lower socioeconomic (SES) areas; it needs to begin educating these students more like how Anyon (1980) observed. Academia needs to treat those from lower SES and juvenile correctional schools like the "elite class" is typically being educated; this means approaching educating this population with innovation and higher expectations. Generalizing this as a more inclusive and effective model of education that was typically reserved for the privileged will likely disrupt the school to prison pipeline. But that remains to be explored.

Secondly, a recommendation stems from the creation of the school to prison pipeline itself. The educational system needs to continue moving away from zero tolerance policies and punitive school discipline. Zero tolerance discipline policies and the school to prison pipeline have a strong relationship, and the bridge between the juvenile justice system and the adult prison system implies a solid connection between the two (The United States Commission on Civil Rights, 2019). Zero tolerance discipline should be reevaluated and replaced with alternative discipline policies. Rather than punitive models, such as detention, suspension, and expulsion, students on the school to prison pipeline need positive interventions that include consistent academic reinforcement and safety. In other words, school needs to provide the similar security nets that gangs provide; schools need to provide security nets that are interwoven fabrics or safety, security, and inclusion. This sense of belonging and security leads to a third observation.

There needs to be a modification in the role correctional education plays in the lives of students regarding rehabilitative services. This modification begins with defining what "rehabilitation" does as practice in correctional facilities today and looking at the actual data that explain what rehabilitation could become. As mentioned above, the data show that education is the best indicator for avoiding recidivism. But this book clearly suggests that education goes beyond books. Education includes knowing and developing life skills to avoid criminality; education includes understanding mental health issues that need to be addressed prior to incarceration. Academic institutions and correctional facilities need to make educational options a priority for the student to understand that a noncriminal life can be achievable, and the criminal life is avoidable. Educational programs in correctional institutions need to provide positive mentorship that goes beyond the walls of incarceration. Mentorship that includes academic and personal mentoring fulfills a key role in positive intervention and development. Ultimately, correctional facilities and education institutions need to work closely together to provide each student-inmate the skills to achieve a good education and the ultimate goal of the noncriminality as part of the rehabilitation process.

The need for intervention for our juveniles on the school to prison pipeline has never been greater. Students living in poverty need to understand that options exist outside of their neighborhoods to strengthen their capacity to prevent the allure of gang life and criminality. Students, especially those on the school to prison pipeline, need the encouragement and academic direction from those within academia that puts the students instead onto the pipeline to college, thus taking the word "prison" out of the lexicon entirely. For incarcerated students, there need to be the positive interventions from academia that become the norm and to redirect them from the school to prison pipeline, a path which would more than likely lead them to adult incarceration facilities long term.

Currently, universities and community colleges are vamping up programs that are directed toward the incarcerated adult, but the universities and community colleges need to place more of an emphasis on incarcerated juvenile education to stop the pathway from juvenile hall to adult prison. This is being done locally. The same juvenile hall where the students began the relationship and a local community college are taking what we learned from this pilot to create a program that gives the incarcerated juveniles positive education options that could help mitigate their negative high school experiences, including for-credit, in-person classes that seek to prepare them academically for life after incarceration. The college program focuses on a culturally relevant and critical education experience to highlight the experiences the student-inmates can bring to the academic experience. Providing the culturally responsive and critical education provides the incarcerated students positivity over all the negativity that has been experienced in their academic trajectory.

Likewise, the local university has developed a partnership with a local non-profit organization (NPO) and a satellite juvenile hall site to provide postsecondary classes to adjudicated and formerly incarcerated juveniles that follows the findings: a strong collaboration between incarcerated juveniles, current higher education staff, and academic administration can find a positive academic experience. Moreover, it can enhance their current academic experience. In the university, the students will be granted conditional admission and have full student status. They will have all the rights and responsibilities as students who attend at the main university campus. The program will continue to develop using further research and findings to provide the best possible rehabilitative educational pathway for incarcerated and formerly incarcerated students.

With the creation of this and other educational opportunities, higher education programs in juvenile justice facilities can inspire a more positive outlook about higher education for incarcerated students and current formerly incarcerated students. In addition, following the model of finding and recognizing the student voice, institutions of higher education should continue to capture data about the positive impact that such a program can have for incarcerated students. Also, given the powerful outcomes inherent in the Arts Based Research approaches, the students and the higher education faculty could jointly reflect on their experiences through both academic and creative outlets in future work. This would allow future participants of higher education to express their mutual growth and development in reimagining this form of education. Through ongoing research, we could continue to build on the limited data that exists in the short-term, as well as provide the opportunity for longitudinal studies. These studies can help us learn better ways to bridge the gap than currently exists between this group and their academic success and eliminate the bridge that exists between juvenile hall and adult prison. Academia should not lose sight of this marginalized population as they attempt to diversify campuses and provide educational opportunities. Ultimately, it is my hope that existing negative impressions about incarcerated youth could be reversed, so that they can show the world their up to now untapped potential in the academic milieu.

DISRUPTING THE SCHOOL TO PRISON PIPELINE

Education, as a whole, needs to take responsibility, especially with the growing research and data on the school to prison pipeline. If education knows the obvious school to prison pipeline data, then there must be actions in place to disrupt the school to prison pipeline. Thankfully, programs and methods of disruption are emerging to stop the cycle of juvenile incarceration and the role education plays in the school to prison pipeline. The purpose of disrupting the school to prison pipeline aims to stop the intentional imprisonment of marginal peoples, for there are "over two million poor, mentally ill, under- or uneducated, nongender conforming, noncitizens, and/or non-white" (Meiners, 2011, p. 549). Reigniting the fire and encouraging the benefits of education needs to be the first step in reducing recidivism. This is done in two ways. First, legislation at the school and government level needs to address the concerning school to prison pipeline. Second, programs designed to address the educational needs of incarcerated juveniles need to be educationally focused by honoring the voice of incarcerated and formerly incarcerated juveniles. Both attend to deeply rooted racial inequities; both will bring the necessary people—teachers, administrators, students, and officials—to create a movement. For the collaboration programs that are brought together between the juvenile justice systems and institutions of higher education, they all need to set out to create a movement.

The learning curve, meaning the time it takes to get their voice, with the students is long and slow, but it is an ascending curve. The progression of learning was the essential motivating factor during the time of writing and reflecting on this text; even more, it was an essential motivating factor for the formerly incarcerated students who were involved in the program. Once they began to experience a traditional higher education, incorporating Culturally Responsive Teaching, Funds of Knowledge, and the emergence of voice, the students became scholars. They experienced guest speakers; in fact, there were so many professors asking to speak to our group that we had to turn away some professors. Overall, with the emergence of voice, they were showing that they were academics. I recalled an old TED Talk by Sir Ken Robinson—"How to escape education's Death Valley." He was right, and we had a class of incarcerated juveniles who proved exactly what he was saying: the student's mind was not dead; it was dormant. We watered their academic curiosity, and watched the curiosity grow like to poppies in the middle of the desert. As the higher education program indicates, incarcerated students can be educated, especially when they are given curriculum reserved for other students. Thus, we can reverse the school to prison pipeline to create a Corrections to College Pipeline.

Reversing the school to prison pipeline does not happen in the classroom only. It also happens in the courtroom. Three legislative issues can be passed to help disrupt the school to prison pipeline. The first legislative issue revolves around the Gang Abatement and Prevention Act (GAPA). GAPA focuses on increasing law enforcement to deter gang crime and gang prevention by expanding the definition of the term "gang" and "gang crime," increasing the penalties for gang-related activities, and increasing funding to local agencies to help deter and prosecute gang-related crime (Boyd, 2009). The loosely based language of GAPA allows for schools and school districts to determine minor instances, such as a physical altercation between two students of color, to be defined as gang activity. Secondly, the Every Student Succeeds Act (ESSA) needs an overhaul. This law created amendments to Title I to strengthen reentry programs, but reentry needs to focus on

- "Requiring education planning, credit transfer, and timely re-enrollment in the appropriate educational placements for youth transitioning between correctional facilities and local agencies and programs";
- "Requiring correctional facilities receiving funds under the law to coordinate educational services with local educational agencies upon a young person's reentry so as to minimize education and achievement disruption"; and
- "Supporting targeted services for youth who have come into contact with both the child welfare and juvenile justice systems" (National Juvenile Justice Network, 2011).

The most pressing legislative issue remains the "zero tolerance" policy help by schools and school districts. Whereas zero tolerance aims to punish infractions that can be defined as loosely as the GAPA language, agencies such as the United States Attorney General's office, the American Academy of Pediatrics, and the American Psychological Association have concluded zero tolerance as ineffective and harmful (Mallett, 2016). In addition, Mallett (2016) notes that student codes of conduct are not responsive to the individual and are focused on punishment versus rehabilitation.

A true disruption to the school to prison pipeline relies on creating effective educational programs for the people who fall victim to the school to prison pipeline. In 1954, the United States Supreme Court noted: "it is doubtful that any child may reasonably be expected to succeed in life if he is denied the opportunity to an education" in its *Brown v. Board of Education* ruling. Incarcerated juveniles struggle with not spending enough time in school in order become academically successful, so interagency programs can strengthen communication and be helpful in keeping students in school (Feierman, Levick, & Mody, 2010). Programs, or alternatives to the carceral state, create power networks and often construct alternatives to being adjudicated (Meiners, 2011). Warren (2019) writes, "Research shows that positive behavior intervention and supports and other alternatives . . . can herald a larger transformation of school climate" (p. 3). For example, many forms of school to prison pipeline disruptions can be created: diversion programs, restorative justice programs, enhanced alternative education programs—including postsecondary education. The following is a list (Shippen, Patterson, Green, & Smitherman, 2012) and brief summation of programs:

1. Diversion Programs: usually court ordered to reduce incarceration via screening and assessment and direct juveniles to necessary interventions.
2. Restorative Justice: a method of bringing together victims and offenders to reach a collective agreement to correct past wrong-doings and identify accountability
3. Enhanced Alternative Education: academically centered programs that attempt to reduce the amount of youth who enter the school to prison pipeline

Increasing programs, or alternatives, increases engagement by the students and stakeholders; thus, creating a school to prison pipeline disruption (Shippen et al., 2012). Schools can, then, participate in providing an appropriate education for incarcerated juveniles by promoting programs—before the courts get involved—to supplement education and encourage all stakeholders to become involved (Feierman et al., 2010).

CONCLUSION

The time to reflect on the educational experience of the incarcerated juvenile is now. The sense of urgency to advocate for incarcerated juvenile's educational experience exists because there is an unknown about what may emerge due to the current political climate combined with precedence (Giroux, 2009). Little has been done to change a historical disservice to the majority people of color and society directing them into incarceration via a purposeful negative educational experience. Legislation has continued the postbellum perpetuation of criminality with trumped up public mis-speculation about race-based street crime, socioeconomics, and educational disservice (Heiner, 2016).

Facilities offering juvenile justice education need to focus on the student; in addition, the administrators and teacher in the facilities need to have the understanding that the student are incarcerated for a variety of reasons. Nonetheless, it is the final stop for the students unless the barrier between criminality and education is broken; there is a likely probability the student will return to jail, or worse, enter the adult incarceration system (Kollhoff, 2002). If the student reenters the criminal justice system, they will join a racialized system (Annamma, 2016) that essentially welcomes their presence.

Finding and developing learning strategies and curriculum, then, becomes one of the primary responsibilities for juvenile justice education. According to Winn and Behizadeh (2011), "the decline of academic rigor in schools has contributed to the culture of the school-to-prison pipeline" (p. 151). Students who experience incarceration tend to experience less than adequate educational rigor; in other words, school has given up the student. The inverse is also true: the student, then, gives up on school.

If the student and school have abandoned hope of the efficacy of education, this leaves everyone in a precarious predicament and makes everyone callous over time. But the pedagogical fire can be reignited through a Culturally Responsive Teaching and Funds of Knowledge approach. Barnes and Motz (2018) found that policies making teachers aware of the emerging prejudices can seize negative inferences about race, especially in classroom management. Teachers can experience settings that ask them to adjust the curriculum and pedagogy successfully. The challenging practice of academic adjustment becomes a practice in diversity sensitivity, professionalism, and pedagogy (Wade, Bohac, & Platt, 2013), making the outdated method of education for juvenile justice education obsolete. This is a system where little regard was given to knowledge and skill but continued the negative cycle by arbitrarily placing students in classroom based on the previous year's grade level (Foley, 2001).

The prejudices that exist in education are certain but making sure the institution recognizes its partialities is the first step in putting an end to the school to prison pipeline. Disrupting the school to prison pipeline is the underlying focus of the research. Daiute (2016, p. 134) notes, "organizations, whether nongovernmental organizations, civil society organizations, or grass roots movements, have a major presence in the lives of young people . . . , especially in situations of political violence and transition where state-run organizations like public schools are in disarray." Providing youth—on the school to prison pipeline—places to address psychological and academic help is one step in disrupting the school to prison pipeline. Additionally, groups allow youth on the school to prison pipeline to recognize they have a voice. Voice stops the exclusionary and expulsionary practices that typically pushes the students into the school to prison pipeline (Ross, 2016), but giving voice keeps the student off the same tortuous track.

Educators and legislatures need to consider the social justice lens when working with and working for incarcerated juveniles. Milner, Cunningham, O'Connor, and Kestenberg (2018) point out that students, especially those on the school to prison pipeline track, need the following:

- Co-constructed classrooms;
- Academically and psychologically safe classrooms;
- Academic and behavioral boundaries;
- Learning;
- Diverse pedagogical practices that embrace learning.

Students experiencing juvenile justice education need the opportunity to succeed, and the opportunity does not exist in the "business as usual" attitude.

References

Abrams, L. S., & Terry, D. L. (2014). "You can run but you can't hide": How formerly incarcerated young men navigate neighborhood risks. *Children and Youth Services Review*, *47*(P1), 61–69. doi:10.1016/j.childyouth.2014.03.012.

Allen-DeBoer, R. A., Malmgren, K. W., & Glass, M.-E. (2006). Reading Instruction for Youth With Emotional and Behavioral Disorders in a Juvenile Correctional Facility. *Behavioral Disorders*, *32*(1), 18–28.

American Academy of Child and Adolescent Psychiatry. (n.d.). Teen brain: Behavior, problem solving, and decision making. Retrieved November 12, 2021, from https://www.aacap.org/AACAP/Families_and_Youth/Facts_for_Families/FFF-Guide/The-Teen-Brain-Behavior-Problem-Solving-and-Decision-Making-095.aspx.

American Academy of Child & Adolescent Psychiatry. (2016). *Teen brain: Behavior, problem solving, and decision making*. Retrieved from https://www.aacap.org/Families_and_Youth/Facts_for_Families/FFF-Guide/The-Teen-Brain-Behavior-Problem-Solving-and-Decision-Making-095.aspx.

Annamma, S. (2016). Disrupting the carceral state through education journey mapping. *International Journal of Qualitative Studies in Education (QSE)*, *29*(9), 1210–1230.

Annamma, S., Morrison, D., & Jackson, D. (2014). Disproportionality fills in the gaps: Connections between achievement, discipline and special education in the school-to-prison pipeline. *Berkeley Review of Education*, *5*(1), 53–87.

Anyon, J. (1980). Social class and the hidden curriculum of work. In G. Handel, & G. Handel (Eds.), *Childhood socialization* (pp. 369–394). New Brunswick, NJ: Aldine Transaction.

Baltonado, H. M., Harris, P. J., & Rutherford, R. B. (2005). Academic achievement in juvenile corrections: Examining the impact of age, ethnicity and disability. *Education & Treatment of Children*, *28*(4), 361–379.

Barnes, J. C., & Motz, R. T. (2018). Reducing racial inequalities in adulthood arrest by reducing inequalities in school discipline: Evidence from the school-to-prison pipeline. *Developmental Psychology*, *54*(12), 2328–2340.

Barone, T., & Eisner, E. (2012). *Arts Based Research*. Thousand Oaks, CA: Sage Publications.

Barton, A., Corteen, K., Davies, J., & Hobson, A. (2010). Reading the word and reading the world: The impact of a critical pedagogical approach to the teaching of criminology in higher education. *Journal of Criminal Justice Education 21*(1), 24–41. doi: 10.1080/10511250903497917.

Bleakley, P., & Bleakley, C. (2018). School resource officers, "zero tolerance" and the enforcement of compliance in the American education system. *Interchange: A Quarterly Review of Education, 49*(2), 247–261.

Blomberg, T. G., Bales, W. D., Mann, K., Piquero, A. R., & Berk, R. A. (2011). Incarceration, education and transition from delinquency. *Journal of Criminal Justice, 39*(4), 355–365. doi:10.1016/j.jcrimjus.2011.04.003.

Bourdieu, P., & Passeron, J. C. (1990). *Reproduction in education, society, and culture*. London: Sage.

Boyd, T. M. (2009). Confronting racial disparity: Legislative responses to the school-to-prison pipeline. *Harvard Civil Rights-Civil Liberties Law Review, 44*(2), 571–580.

Cahnmann-Taylor, M., & Siegesmund, R. (2008) *Arts Based Research in education: Foundations for practice*. New York: Routledge.

Cammarota, J. (2011). From hopelessness to hope: Social justice pedagogy in urban education and youth development. *Urban Education, 46*(4), 828–844. doi: 10.1177/0042085911399931.

Carbado, D. W., & Roithmayr, D. (2014). Critical race theory meets social science. *Annual Review of Law & Social Science, 10*(5), 149–167.

Center on Juvenile and Criminal Justice. (2019). *The San Francisco industrial school and the origins of juvenile justice in California: A glance at the great reformation*. Retrieved from http://www.cjcj.org/news/6012.

Chavez, V., & Soep, E. (2005). Youth radio and the pedagogy of collegiality. *Harvard Educational Review, 75*(4), 409–434.

Chomsky, N., & Edward, H. (1988). *Manufacturing consent*. New York: Pantheon Publishing.

Clandinin, D. J. (2013). *Engaging in narrative inquiry*. New York: Routledge.

Crotty, M. (1998). *Foundations of social research: Meaning and perspective in the research process*. Sydney, Australia: Allen & Unwin.

Daiute, C. (2016). A Relational Approach to Human Development Research and Practice in 21st Century Violence and Displacement. *Human Development (0018716X), 59*(2/3), 128–151.

Darder, A. (2015). *Freire and education*. New York: Routledge.

Dewey, J. (1934). *Art as experience*. New York: The Berkley Publishing Group.

Dimitriadis, G., & Carlson, D. (2003). Special issue: Aesthetics, popular presentation, and democratic public pedagogy. *Cultural Studies/Critical Methodologies, 3*(1), 3–7.

Eisner, E. W. (2008). Art and knowledge. In J. Knowles & A. L. Cole (Eds.), *Handbook of the arts in qualitative research: Perspectives, methodologies, examples, and issues* (p. 3–12). Thousand Oaks, CA: Sage.

Elias, M. (2013). The School-to-Prison Pipeline. *Teaching Tolerance*, 52(43), 39–40.

Ezell, M., & Levy, M. (2003). An evaluation of an arts program for incarcerated juvenile offenders. *Journal of Correctional Education, 54*(3), 108–114.

Feierman, J., Levick, M., & Mody, A. (2009). The school-to-prison pipeline . . . and back: Obstacles and remedies for the re-enrollment of adjudicated youth. *New York Law School Law Review, 54*(4), 1115–1129.

Foucault, M. (1977). *Discipline and punish: The birth of the prison.* New York: Vintage Books.

Foley, R. (2001). Academic characteristics of incarcerated youth and correctional educational programs: A literature review. *Journal of Emotional and Behavioral Disorders, 9*(4), 248–259.

Freire, P. (1970). *Pedagogy of the oppressed.* New York: Continuum.

Friedman, A. (2003). Juveniles held hostage for profit by CSC in Florida. In T. Herivel & P. Wright (Eds.), *Prison nation: The warehousing of America's poor* (pp. 154–155). New York: Taylor & Francis Books.

Furman, R., Langer, C. L., Davis, C. S., Gallardo, H. P., & Kulkarni, S. (2007). Expressive, research and reflective poetry as qualitative inquiry: A study of adolescent identity. *Qualitative Research, 7*(3), 301–315.

Gadsen, V. L. (2008). The arts and education: Knowledge generation, pedagogy, and the discourse of learning. *Review of Research in Education, 32*(1), 29–61.

Gagnon, J. C., Barber, B. R., Van Loan, C., & Leone, P. E. (2009). Juvenile correctional schools: Characteristics and approaches to curriculum. *Education & Treatment of Children, 32*(4), 673–696.

Giroux, H. A. (2008) Education and the crisis of youth: Schooling and the promise of democracy. *The Educational Forum, 73*(1), 8–18. doi: 10.1080/00131720802539523.

Giroux, H. A., & Giroux, S. S. (2006). Challenging neoliberalism's new world order: The promise of critical pedagogy. *Cultural Studies/Critical Methodologies, 6*(1), 21–32. doi:10.1177/1532708605282810.

Goldkind, L. (2011). A leadership opportunity for school social workers: Bridging the gaps in school reentry for juvenile justice system youths. *Children & Schools, 33*(4), 229–239.

González, N., & Moll, L. C. (2002). Cruzando el Puente: Building Bridges to Funds of Knowledge. *Educational Policy, 16*(4), 623–642.

Gosden, N. P., Kramp, P., Gabrielsen, G., Andersen, T. F., & Sestoft, D. (n.d.). Violence of Young Criminals Predicts Schizophrenia: A 9-Year Register-Based Followup of 15-to 19-Year Old Criminals. Academic.oup.com. Retrieved January 30, 2022, from https://academic.oup.com/schizophreniabulletin/article/31/3/759/1894407.

Gregory, A., Skiba, R. J., & Noguera, P. A. (2010). The achievement gap and the discipline gap: Two sides of the same coin? *Educational Researcher, 39*(1), 59–68.

Griffin, K. W., Botvin, G. J., Scheier, L. M., Diaz, T., & Miller, N. L. (2000). Parenting practices as predictors of substance use, delinquency, and aggression among urban minority youth: Moderating effects of family structure and gender. *Psychology of Addictive Behaviors, 14*(2), 174–184.

Heiner, B. (2016). The procedural entrapment of mass incarceration. *Philosophy & Social Criticism, 42*(6), 594–631.

Heitzeg, N. A. (2009). Education or incarceration: Zero tolerance policies and the school to prison pipeline. *Forum on Public Policy Online, 2009*(2), 1–21.

Hockenberry, S., Sickmund, M., & Sladky, A. (2009). Juvenile residential facilities census, 2006: Selected findings. *Juvenile Offenders and Victims: National Report Series Bulletin.* Washington, DC: Office of Juvenile Justice and Delinquency Prevention.

Houchins, D. E., Jolivette, K., Krezmien, M. P., & Baltodano, H. M. (2008). A multi-state study examining the impact of explicit reading instruction with incarcerated students. *Journal of Correctional Education, 59*(1), 65–85.

Hytten, K., & Bettez, S. C. (2011). Understanding education for social justice. *Educational Foundations, 25*(1), 7–24.

Irizarry, J. G., & Raible, J. (2014). "A Hidden Part of Me": Latino/a students, silencing, and the epidermalization of inferiority. *Equity & Excellence in Education, 47*(4), 430–444.

Jacobi, T. (2008). Writing for change: Engaging juveniles through alternative literacy education. *Journal of Correctional Education, 59*(2), 71–93.

Jones, K., Ferguson, A., Ramirez, C., & Owens, M. (2018). Seen but not heard: Personal narratives of systematic failure within the school-to-prison pipeline. *Taboo: The Journal of Culture and Education, 17*(4), 49–68.

Jordan, V. S. (2018). The "Imaginary Existence" of black male students. *Penn GSE Perspectives on Urban Education, 15*(1), 1–4.

Kim, J. (2011). Narrative inquiry into (re)imagining alternative schools: A case study of Kevin Gonzales. *International Journal of Qualitative Studies in Education (QSE), 24*(1), 77–96.

Kincheloe, J., & Steinburg, S. (1997). *Changing multiculturalism.* Bristol, PA: Open University Press.

Kollhoff, M. (2002). Juvenile correctional education in the 21st century: Leave no child out. *Journal of Correctional Education, 53*(2), 44–45.

Laajasalo, T., & Hakkanen, H. (n.d.). Excessive violence and psychotic symptomatology among homicide offenders with schizophrenia. *Criminal behaviour and mental health: CBMH.* Retrieved February 3, 2022, from https://pubmed.ncbi.nlm.nih.gov /17143929/.

Ladson-Billings, G. (1995). Toward a theory of culturally relevant pedagogy. *American Education Research Journal, 32*(3), 465–491.

Lahman, M. K. E., Geist, M. R., Rodriguez, K. L., Graglia, P. E., Richard, V. M., & Schendel, R. K. (2010). Poking Around Poetically: Research, Poetry, and Trustworthiness. *Qualitative Inquiry, 16*(1), 39–48.

Leard, D. W., & Lashua, B. (2006). Popular media, critical pedagogy, and inner city youth. *Canadian Journal of Education, 29*(1), 244–264.

Leavy, P. (2013). *Fiction as research practice: Short stories, novellas, and novels.* California: Left Coast Press, Inc.

Leavy, P. (2015). *Method meets art: Arts Based Research practice.* New York: The Guilford Press.

Ledesma, M. C., & Calderon, D. (2015). Critical race theory in education: A review of past literature and a look to the future. *Qualitative Inquiry, 21*(3), 206–222. doi:10.1177/1077800414557825.

Leone, P., & Cutting, C. (2004). Appropriate education, juvenile corrections, and no child left behind. *Behavioral Disorders, 29*(3), 260–265.

Mallett, C. (2016). The school-to-prison pipeline: A critical review of the punitive paradigm shift. *Child & Adolescent Social Work Journal, 33*(1), 15–24. doi:10.1007/s10560-015-0397-1.

Marr, J., Morrissey. (1986). "Bigmouth Strikes Again" [The Smiths]. On *The Queen is Dead*. [LP]. Rough Trade.

McGrew, K. (2016). The dangers of pipeline thinking: How the school-to-prison pipeline metaphor squeezes out complexity. *Educational Theory, 66*(3), 341–367.

McLaren, P. (1998). Revolutionary pedagogy in post-revolutionary times: Rethinking the political economy of critical education. *Educational Theory, 48*(4), 431–462.

McLaren, P. (2003). Critical pedagogy and class struggle in the age of neo-liberal globalization: Notes from history's underside. *Democracy & Nature: The International Journal of Inclusive Democracy. 2003; 9*(1), 65–90. doi: 10.1080/1085566032000074959.

McLaren, P. (2015). *Life in schools: An introduction into critical pedagogy in the foundations of education (6th ed.)*. New York: Paradigm Publications.

Meiners, E. R. (2011). Ending the School-to-Prison Pipeline/Building Abolition Futures. *Urban Review: Issues and Ideas in Public Education, 43*(4), 547–565.

Mennis, J., & Harris, P. (2011). Contagion and repeat offending among urban juvenile delinquents. *Journal of Adolescence, 34*(5), 951–963.

Milner, H. R., IV, Cunningham, H. B., Delale-O'Connor, L., & Kestenberg, E. G. (2018). Are the kids really out of control? Students need support, not punishment. *Educational Leadership, 76*(1), 86–87.

Moll, L. C., Amanti, C., Neff, D., & Gonzalez, N. (1992). Funds of knowledge for teaching: Using a qualitative approach to connect homes and classrooms. *Theory Into Practice, 31*(2), 132–141.

Nance, J. P. (2017). Student surveillance, racial inequalities, and implicit racial bias. *Emory Law Journal, 66*(4), 765–837.

Nayebzadah, R. (2016). The truth behind fiction-based research. *Journal of Humanistic & Social Studies, 7*(2), 49–61.

Nichols, L., Parker, H., & Kruse, M. (n.d.). Nearly three-quarters of youth behind bars suffer from mental health issues. Nearly Three-Quarters of Youth Behind Bars Suffer From Mental Health Issues | *Evident Change*. Retrieved September 28, 2021, from https://www.evidentchange.org/newsroom/news-of-interest/nearly-three-quarters-youth-behind-bars-suffer-mental-health-issues.

Nicholson, C. S., Birchmeier, Z., & Valentine, D. (2009). Exploring the Impact of School Discipline on Racial Disproportion in the Juvenile Justice System. *Social Science Quarterly* (Wiley-Blackwell), *90*(4), 1003–1018.

Nocella, A. J., II, Parmar, P., & Stovall, D. (2018). *From Education to Incarceration: Dismantling the School-to-Prison Pipeline, Second Edition*. Peter Lang Publishing Group.

Nuño, L. E., & Katz, C. M. (2019). Understanding Gang Joining from a Cross Classified Multi-Level Perspective. *Deviant Behavior, 40*(3), 301–325.

Office of Juvenile Justice and Delinquency Prevention. (2018). *Reentry starts here: A guide for youth in long-term juvenile corrections and treatment programs.* Retrieved from http://ojjdp.ojp.gov/sites/g/files/xyckuh176/files/pubs/251193.pdf.

Percer, L. H. (2002). Going Beyond the Demonstrable Range in Educational Scholarship: Exploring the Intersections of Poetry and Research. *The Qualitative Report, 7*(2), 1–13. https://doi.org/10.46743/2160-3715/2002.1983.

Platt, J. S., Casey, R. E., & Faessel, R. T. (2006).The need for a paradigmatic change in juvenile correctional education. *Preventing School Failure, 51*(1), 31–38.

Porno For Pyros. (1993). "Packin' 25" [Recorder by Porno For Pyros]. On *Porno For Pyros* [LP]. Warner Bros. Records.

Potter, H., Boggs, B., Dunbar, C. (2017). Discipline and punishment: How schools are building the school-to-prison pipeline. In N. Okilwa, M. Khalifa, & F. Briscoe (Eds.), *The school to prison pipeline: The role of culture and discipline in school.* Bingley, UK: Emerald Publishing Limited.

Prendergast, M. (2009). Introduction: The phenomena of poetry in research. In M. Prendergast & P. Sameshima (Eds.), *Poetic Inquiry: Vibrant voices in the social sciences* (pp. xix–xlii). Netherlands: Sense Publishers.

Risler, E., & O'Rourke, T. (2009). Thinking exit at entry: Exploring outcomes of Georgia's juvenile justice educational programs. *Journal of Correctional Education, 60*(3), 225–239.

Ross, C. J. (2016). "Bitch," go directly to jail: Student speech and entry into the school-to-prison pipeline. *Temple Law Review, 88*(4), 717–740.

Sanchez, A. E. (2019). In spite of prison. *Harvard Law Review, 132*(6), 1650–1683.

Sanders, C. (2021). State juvenile justice reforms can boost opportunity, particularly for communities of color. Center on Budget and Policy Priorities. Retrieved January 3, 2022, from https://www.cbpp.org/research/state-budget-and-tax/state-juvenile-justice-reforms-can-boost-opportunity-particularly-for.

Schwartz, J. (2015). After incarceration and adult learning: A collaborative inquiry and writing project. *Adult Learning, 26*(2), 51–58.

Shapiro, J. (2004). Can poetry be data? Potential relationships between poetry and research. *Families, Systems & Health: The Journal of Collaborative Family HealthCare, 22*(2), 171–177.

Shippen, M. E., Patterson, D., Green, K. L., & Smitherman, T. (2012). Community and school practices to reduce delinquent behavior: Intervening on the school-to-prison pipeline. *Teacher Education and Special Education, 35*(4), 296–308.

Smith, L. T. (1999). *Decolonizing methodologies: Research and indigenous peoples.* London: Zed Books.

Stinson, A. (2009). A review of cultural art programs and outcomes for at-risk youths. *Best Practice in Mental Health, 5*(1), 10–25.

Suspensions and expulsions. EdData. (2019, June 6). Retrieved January 8, 2022, from https://www.ed-data.org/article/Suspensions-and-Expulsions.

Thompson, J. (2016). Eliminating zero tolerance policies in schools: Miami-Dade county public schools' approach. *Brigham Young University Education & Law*

Journal, 2016(2), 325–349. Retrieved from https://papers.ssrn.com/sol3/papers .cfm?abstract_id=2820411.

Tyner, A. R. (2014). The emergence of the school-to-prison pipeline. Retrieved from https://www.americanbar.org/groups/gpsolo/publications/gpsolo_ereport /2014/june_2014/the_emergence_of_the_school-to-prison_pipeline/.

Underwood, L. A., & Washington, A. (2017). Mental illness and juvenile offenders. *The Encyclopedia of Juvenile Delinquency and Justice*, 1–8. https://doi.org/10 .1002/9781118524275.ejdj0146.

United States Department of Education Office for Civil Rights. (2014). *Civil rights data collection data snapshot: School discipline*. Retrieved from https://ocrdata.ed .gov/assets/downloads/CRDC-School-Discipline-Snapshot.pdf.

United States Department of Education. (2012). *A reentry education model: Supporting education and career advancement for low-skill individuals in corrections*. Retrieved from http://www.ed.gov/about/offices/list/ovae/pi/AdultEd/ correctional/education.html#4.

Vaught, S. E. (2013). Hate speech in a juvenile male prison school and in US schooling. *Urban Review: Issues and Ideas in Public Education, 44*(2), 239–264.

Wade, W., Bohac, P., & Platt, J. S. (2013). Technology-based induction: Professional development strategies for correctional education. *Journal of Correctional Education, 64*(3), 22–36.

Wald, J., & Losen, D. J. (2003) Defining and redirecting a school-to-prison pipeline. *New Directions for Youth Development, 2003*(99), 9–15.

Warren, M. (2019, January 22). Parents must shut down the school-to-prison pipeline. *The American Prospect*. Retrieved October 11, 2021, from https://prospect.org/ justice/parents-must-shut-school-to-prison-pipeline/.

Winn, M. T. (2010). "Our side of the story": Moving incarcerated youth voices from margins to center. *Race, Ethnicity and Education, 13*(3), 313–325.

Winn, M. T., & Behizadeh, N. (2011). The right to be literate: Literacy, education and the school-to-prison pipeline. *Review of Research in Education, 35*(1), 147–173.

Index

About the Author

Dr. Gregory Barraza has been a teacher, professor, and administrator in alternative and correctional education for over twenty-five years. During his tenure, he has worked with the most vulnerable students in Orange County, including security risk, maximum security students, and students with emotional and physical disabilities. In addition to his teaching, he is Coordinator of Inmate Education for Santa Ana College's Centennial Education Center at the federal level. In his spare time, he is an adjunct professor at Chapman University, Attallah College of Educational Studies and Director of the Underground Panthers Juvenile Lifers Reentry Educational Program. His areas of interest are the efficacy of correctional education and juvenile justice education, specifying on the social and cultural influences that influence and lead to the school to prison pipeline. He is on the continuous fight for advocating for education improvement and empowerment for incarcerated and justice impacted individuals.

www.ingramcontent.com/pod-product-compliance
Lightning Source LLC
Chambersburg PA
CBHW021842290326
41932CB00064B/1235